LAKE DISTRICT UNLOCKED

by

Deborah Done

illustrations by

Katherine Hardy

edited by

Emily Kerr & Joshua Perry

NOTES

This book belongs to:

_____

CONTENTS

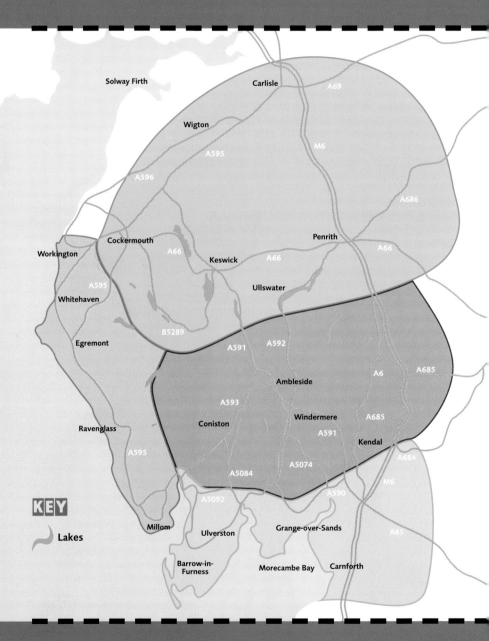

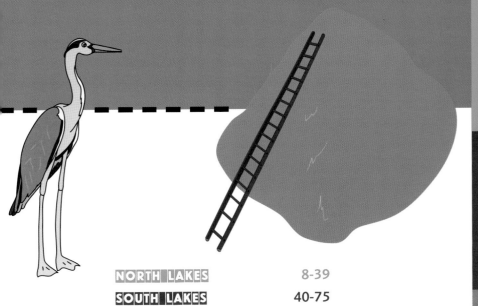

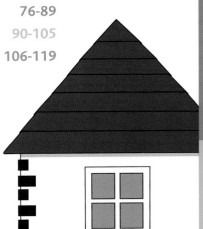

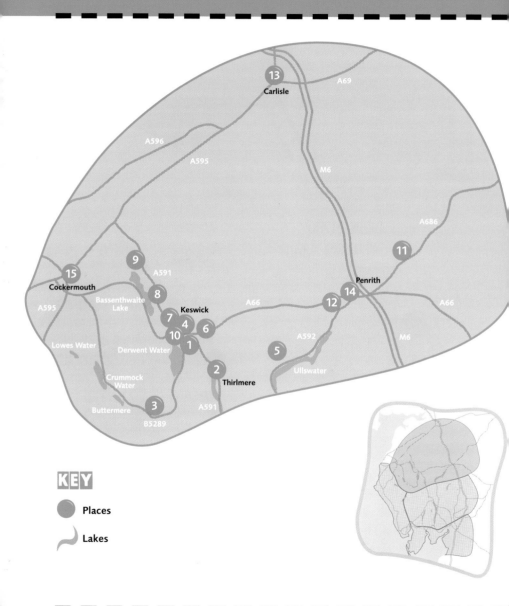

KEY

● Places

〜 Lakes

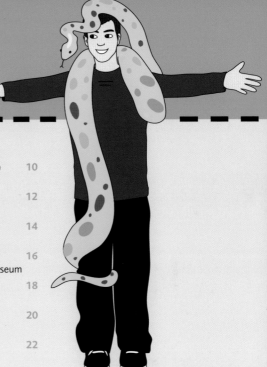

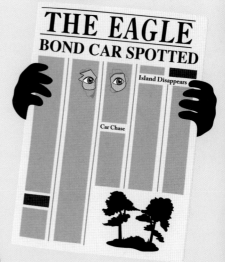

BALANCE A BOULDER ON YOUR FINGERTIP

...at the Bowder Stone

Unless you want to be squished we strongly suggest you don't actually try to balance a 2,000 tonne stone on your fingertip! But, by using camera trickery, you can create a pretty convincing photo.

The extraordinary Bowder Stone in the Borrowdale Valley is the largest standing stone in the Lake District. At ten metres high and sixteen metres wide it is bigger than a terraced house! Incredibly, it somehow balances on one corner, giving the impression that it could topple over any second.

Stand beneath the stone and reach up to touch it. You will create the illusion that you are balancing the boulder on your fingertip! There's also a ladder resting against the stone so that you can climb up and sit on top of it.

Sticker Scores

5 BRILLIANT BOULDER

4 SUPER STONE

3 MYSTERIOUS MOUND

2 REASONABLE ROCK

1 PATHETIC PEBBLE

Make A Day Of It

🔑 Stroll up to the Lodore Falls, a nearby waterfall. The series of cascades drop over 60 metres and are particularly impressive after heavy rain.

🔑 See if you can spot the ruined fort on Castle Crag in the Borrowdale Valley, probably used by ancient Britons to defend themselves against Roman invaders.

🔑 Stop off for a snack at beautiful Grange-in-Borrowdale. There are some lovely tea gardens in a 200 year old building.

← Stairway up a stone

What came after the Stone Age and the Bronze Age?

The saus-age!

Fascinating Facts

⭐ **The Bowder Stone is known by geologists as a perched rock. It was transported to Borrowdale from a long way away (probably from Scotland) on a glacier. When the glaciers melted at the end of the Ice Age it 'perched' in its current lopsided position. So, as it's been that way for thousands of years you can be reassured that it's pretty safe!**

⭐ Victorians, who loved visiting the stone, believed it had tumbled down from the crags above. Mind you, the Victorians also believed that a good way to cure disease was by draining blood from someone's body, so they're probably not the most reliable source of information!

PLAN YOUR VISIT 1

Bowder Stone
Near Grange-in-Borrowdale, Keswick, Cumbria
www.visitcumbria.com/kes/bowder.htm

FREE

I want to go here ☐

11

SPOT A RED SQUIRREL

...at Thirlmere Reservoir

Red squirrels are native to Britain but sadly they are in danger of extinction. Cumbria is one of their last strongholds in the UK – and the forest around Thirlmere is one of several refuges set up to protect them.

Thirlmere is an ideal home for red squirrels. The forest contains lots of conifer trees, which provide plenty of seeds for them to chomp on. And the forest managers have given the reds a helping hand – rope bridges have been installed across the roads to help the squirrels get across safely!

Follow the signs to the willow hide near Swirls car park. Squirrel yourself away in a quiet spot and keep your eyes peeled for tufty-eared creatures . . .

Sticker Scores

5	4	3
HAZELNUTS	CHESTNUTS	BEECH NUTS

2	1
PEANUTS	GONE NUTS

Make A Day Of It

Visit a submerged village at the southern end of Thirlmere. When the reservoir was created from two smaller lakes in 1890, Wythburn village was totally covered in water. Today only the church and a few houses remain. We hope they told the people who lived there before they flooded it!

Photo Op

Red squirrels look amazing when photographed well, but it's not easy to do. Make as little noise as possible when you're preparing for your snap and with a bit of luck you'll get a good one.

Fascinating Facts

★ Red squirrels have been in the UK for 10,000 years. However, they are now at risk of extinction because of the threat from grey squirrels. Greys are the reds' bigger, scary cousins. They were introduced into England in the late 1800s and have since swept across the country, causing reds to disappear. Greys carry a virus (squirrelpox) which kills the poor reds. They also take their food just to really annoy them. Meanies.

★ Red squirrels frequently feature in Lake District books and art. Beatrix Potter imagined Squirrel Nutkin from her home here (see p56), and Dalemain House has a picture of a red squirrel in every room (see p32). Oh, and we've got one on our cover!

PLAN YOUR VISIT ②

Thirlmere Reservoir
Near Keswick, Cumbria
www.visitcumbria.com/kes/thirlm.htm

`FREE`

I want to go here ☐

← Squirrels this way!

United Utilities Permitted Footpath

ROCK CLIMB AT A SLATE MINE

...at Honister Slate Mine

Honister is a working slate mine, selling fireplaces and kitchen tops. But don't worry – we're not suggesting you buy a work surface. You'll want to go there because they also offer sky-high rock climbing trips!

Honister's Via Ferrata (an Italian expression for 'Iron Way') is a clever adventure climbing system. It's the first and only one in England. You clamber along the rock face while attached to it by a cable and harness.

The highest point is 600 metres up in the air, and from here you'll have the sort of view you'd normally only get from an aeroplane. Miners during Victorian times used this route (without ropes) as a short cut to get to work. We'd rather stick to the bus!

Sticker Scores

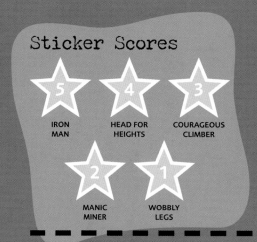

5 — IRON MAN

4 — HEAD FOR HEIGHTS

3 — COURAGEOUS CLIMBER

2 — MANIC MINER

1 — WOBBLY LEGS

Best Of The Rest

🔑 You need to be ten years old and at least 1.3 metres tall to climb the Via Ferrata, but there are lots of other great experiences at Honister if this rules you out. It's the last working slate mine in Britain and you can take an underground tour to see how it all works. With a miner's helmet on your head and a lamp in your hand you can explore miles of mining tunnels and caves deep under the ground.

> **What did the mountain climber name his son?**
> Cliff!

← DON'T LOOK DOWN . . . .

Fascinating Facts

★ **Slate is a form of rock that is popular for things like roofing tiles and work surfaces. It was formed long before dinosaurs walked on the earth and can come in all sorts of colours from grey to purple.**

★ Lakeland slate is a unique green colour and is used in local Lakeland roofs and houses. It's considered so beautiful and hard-wearing that it's also been used in Buckingham Palace, the Ritz Hotel and Scotland Yard in London. Look out for it while you're exploring.

★ **The Victorian workers had to make do with candles to light the tunnels and hand tools to cut through the slate. It was hard work and very dangerous.**

PLAN YOUR VISIT ③

Honister Slate Mine
Honister Pass, Borrowdale, Keswick, CA12 5XN
www.honister-slate-mine.co.uk

📞 **01768 777230**

🕘 **Daily 09.00-17.00**

£££ (Via Ferrata)

££ (Underground Tour)

I want to go here ☐

SPY ON JAMES BOND'S CARS

...at Cars of the Stars and the Bond Museum

Where can you find the Batmobile, Fred Flintstone's Stone Age banger and the flying Ford Anglia from the *Harry Potter* films side by side? Not in your local car park, but at Cars of the Stars in Keswick!

The museum is *traffic* jam-packed with vehicles from TV and film. They're displayed as they were on the original film sets, so they're set in muddy battlefields, bomb sites, villages and towns. *James Bond* fans are in for a particular treat – the museum's giant collection of Bond cars is now so big that they've moved them into a separate building nearby.

THE EAGLE
BOND CAR SPOTTED

Island Disappears

Car Chase

Sticker Scores

5	**4**	**3**
SUPER SPY	DOUBLE AGENT	INTELLIGENT INVESTIGATOR

2	**1**
ORDINARY OPERATIVE	PC PLOD

Many of the films' gadgets and costumes are also on show – including the original golden gun. Prepare to be **shaken** *and* **stirred**!

Best Of The Rest

🔑 Keswick holds a great market on Saturdays, where you can shop for food, clothes and books. It's been running since the 1200s (but luckily the stalls have changed since then!).

🔑 Visit the Keswick Museum and Art Gallery. They have an odd mixture of exhibits, including a 600 year old stuffed cat, Napoleon's teacup and a spoon made from the leg bone of a sheep!

← Tanks for visiting!

Fascinating Facts

★ **Keswick is an old English word for cheese farm. The name came from the fact that the town's market used to sell lots of the yellow stuff.**

★ James Bond's favourite car is an Aston Martin – the British gentleman's sports car. However, when caught in a sticky situation he's been known to experiment with all kinds of other vehicles. At the Bond Museum you'll find a **tank** (from *Goldeneye*), a **jetpack** (from *Thunderball*) and a range of **spytastic speedboats**!

What do you call James Bond in the bath?

Bubble 07!

PLAN YOUR VISIT ④

Cars of the Stars
Standish Street, Keswick, CA12 5LS
www.carsofthestars.com
📞 01768 773757
🕐 Daily 10.00-17.00
(closed some days out of season)
£

The Bond Museum
Southey Hill Trading Estate, Keswick, CA12 5NR
www.thebondmuseum.com
📞 01768 775007
🕐 Daily 10.00-17.00
(closed some days out of season)
£

I want to go here ☐

STAND ABOVE A WATERFALL

...at Aira Force

If you've never seen a real waterfall for yourself, you're in for a treat. At Aira Force a narrow stream of water gushes down the rocks, like a giant toilet that's forever being flushed. (Thankfully, the fast-flowing water is the only thing it has in common with a toilet!)

Aira Force near Ullswater is one of the most spectacular waterfalls in the Lake District. The water drops over twenty metres from top to bottom. That's the same as 35 toilets stacked on top of each other!

After a short climb from the car park you walk up through forest and glades to reach the narrow Aira Beck gorge. Stand on the little stone footbridge that spans the wooded gorge and look down a 21 metre drop at the frothing, tumbling torrent below . . .

Sticker Scores

5 WONDERFUL WATERFALL

4 COMMENDABLE CASCADE

3 SUPERIOR SPOUT

2 REASONABLE RAPID

1 TINY TRICKLE

Which vegetable would you never want in your canoe?

A leek!

Best Of The Rest

 Aira Force lies just north of Ullswater, the second largest lake in the Lake District. There are plenty of activities to enjoy on its shores. You can hire a canoe, go fishing or ride a pony.

 Alternatively head down to the pier at Pooley Bridge and take a trip around the lake on one of the Ullswater Steamers which date from the 1800s.

Top Tip
Tread carefully when approaching the falls as it can get slippery when it rains. And you don't want to end up like Emma!

Fascinating Facts

★ According to legend, a beautiful damsel called Emma was engaged to a knight called Sir Eglamore. While he was away fighting, she sleepwalked to the top of Aira Force. Eglamore returned unexpectedly and touched her arm to wake her as she stood beside the waterfall. Unfortunately she fell into the water and died. *Whoops!* Brokenhearted, he became a monk and lived in a cave, building the little bridge to stop anyone ever stumbling into the falls again.

★ A money tree lies on the ground near the falls. Visitors bash a coin into the tree trunk using a hammer and then make a wish. Who says money doesn't grow on trees?

PLAN YOUR VISIT 5

Aira Force
Ullswater, Cumbria
www.nationaltrust.org.uk

FREE

I want to go here ☐

...at Castlerigg Stone Circle

No one knows why men from the Bronze Age decided to lug enormous volcanic stones up to a lonely moor and place them in a huge circle. Some people think the stones helped them to tell the time, rather like a sundial. If only they'd had watches it might have saved them a lot of hassle!

Castlerigg Stone Circle is the oldest stone circle in England – it was created around 5,000 years ago. Apart from telling the time, suggestions for its original purpose include a trading place, an observatory, or a gathering point for druid ceremonies and sacrifices.

Try to count the stones – legend has it that any two people trying to do so will always end up with a different number!

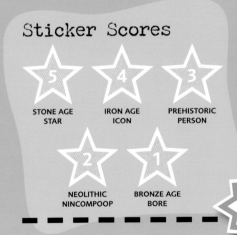

Sticker Scores

⭐ 5 — **STONE AGE STAR**

⭐ 4 — **IRON AGE ICON**

⭐ 3 — **PREHISTORIC PERSON**

⭐ 2 — **NEOLITHIC NINCOMPOOP**

⭐ 1 — **BRONZE AGE BORE**

What's the time?
Time you got
a watch!

Best Of The Rest

🔑 Try to identify the well-known mountains of Helvellyn, Skiddaw and Blencathra nearby. These are some of the highest in Cumbria and all can be spotted from Castlerigg Stone Circle.

🔑 Take a walk from Keswick to the beautiful village of Threlkeld. It's about three miles away along a disused railway line. There you will find the Quarry and Mining Museum, where you will be guided through a metal mine.

Photo Op
Sit on a comfortable-looking stone and pretend to be conducting a mysterious Bronze Age ritual (but not a sacrifice!).

← Bigger than the average watch!

Fascinating Facts

⭐ **The heaviest stone in the Castlerigg Stone Circle weighs 16 tonnes – the same as two adult elephants! So don't try picking it up . . .**

⭐ The highest stone is about 2.3 metres, which is as big as the world's tallest man (or two six year olds standing on top of each other)!

⭐ **Druids were mystical people that lived mainly in parts of the UK and France. Not much is known about them, and they disappeared from history around 2,000 years ago. However, we do know that some druid ceremonies included sacrifices (killing animals or humans to make their gods happy). Actually, maybe it's a good thing they don't exist any more!**

PLAN YOUR VISIT 6

Castlerigg Stone Circle
Near Goosewell Farm, Castlerigg, Near Keswick, Cumbria
www.english-heritage.org.uk

FREE

I want to go here ☐

SEE THE WORLD'S LARGEST PENCIL

...at the Cumberland Pencil Museum

Let's be honest – if you were making a list of exciting subjects for a museum, you wouldn't start with the pencil. So it's a pleasant surprise that the Cumberland Pencil Museum is actually one of the sharpest attractions around!

Pencils are popular in Keswick because graphite (the grey stuff in pencils) was first discovered in nearby Borrowdale. The museum contains a replica of the original graphite mine alongside traditional pencil-making machinery.

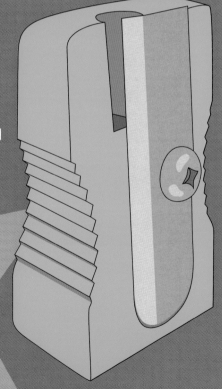

The museum's main attraction is the largest coloured pencil in the world. At almost eight metres long it's twice the length of a boa constrictor (though less likely to squeeze a pig to death). It's made from real pencil materials, so would be ideal for giant doodles – *if* you could pick it up!

Sticker Scores

5 PENCIL MUSEUM

4 FELT-TIP FAIR

3 SHARPENER SHOW

2 ERASER EXHIBITION

1 MUSEUM OF AIR

Best Of The Rest

← The Museum's Big Picture Gallery

🔑 Get creative in the Drawing Zone at the museum. You can try out the Derwent pencils that used to be made here, enter colouring competitions and even draw on the walls. (Don't do that at home though!)

🔑 In the video theatre, watch a clip from the famous Raymond Briggs film *The Snowman*. The film was drawn using Derwent pencils.

🔑 Head to the shop to stock up on top-quality colouring pencils!

Photo Op
Get a snap of you standing in front of the enormous pencil. Hold a normal pencil in your hand to emphasise how big this one is!

Fascinating Facts

⭐ The 'lead' in pencils is in fact not lead at all, but graphite. Graphite, like diamond, is a form of carbon – but that doesn't mean that film stars will be wearing graphite earrings any time soon!

⭐ Making pencils out of lead would not be a very clever idea. Lead is a poisonous metal that can cause stomach pains and brain disorders. And homework is painful enough without the thing you're writing with making you ill too!

⭐ Local legend has it that on a stormy night in the 1500s a tree blew down in Borrowdale to reveal some grey stuff in the ground (graphite). Shepherds started using it to mark their sheep long before its potential for pencils was discovered.

PLAN YOUR VISIT 7

The Cumberland Pencil Museum
Southey Works, Keswick, CA12 5NG
www.pencilmuseum.co.uk

📞 **01768 773626**

🕐 **Daily 09.30-17.00**

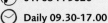

I want to go here ☐

ADMIRE WILD OSPREYS

...in Dodd Wood

The osprey is one of the rarest birds of prey in the UK. In fact they are so rare they were actually extinct in the UK from 1916 to 1954! But don't worry, they are back now, and Dodd Wood is one of the best places to spot them.

With a wingspan of almost two metres and a striking white head, ospreys are spectacular birds. At Dodd Wood, above Bassenthwaite Lake, you can watch them hover, hunt and feed on fish.

The upper viewing point is a thirty minute walk from Dodd Wood car park. From April to September you'll get a great view of the ospreys in action. And if you're lucky you might also spot red squirrels and roe deer here too!

Sticker Scores

5	4	3
BRILLIANT BIRDWATCHER	CARING CONSERVATIONIST	ESTABLISHED ECOLOGIST
2	1	
TRAINEE TWITCHER	BIRD BRAIN	

Make A Day Of It

🔑 The Old Sawmill Tearoom at Dodd Wood is a great place to grab a piece of cake after some serious osprey watching. Alternatively, come here first to pick up walking trail maps for exploring the wood.

🔑 Mirehouse, a stately home opposite the tearooms, is also worth visiting. There are four adventure playgrounds and an a-*maze*-ing heather maze in the grounds!

🔑 Check out the live camera footage of an osprey nest at the Whinatter Visitor Centre. An Osprey Bus links the two sites.

> What birds spend all their time on their knees?
>
> Birds of *pray*!

Fascinating Facts

★ **Ospreys can be found on every continent except Antarctica. They are very faithful animals – breeding pairs usually stay together for life. Awww!**

★ Ospreys only eat fish, and are expert at killing them (they've had a lot of practice). They (the ospreys, not the fish) have razor-sharp eyesight and can spot their prey from a height of 30 metres. They dive down, pull up at the last moment and plunge feet first into the water to grab the fish with their talons. The fish don't really stand a chance!

★ **Ospreys came back to Cumbria in the mid-1990s. In 2001, the first pair to breed in the Lake District for over 150 years reared three chicks at Bassenthwaite. They have returned every summer since.**

PLAN YOUR VISIT 8

Dodd Wood
Near Keswick, Cumbria
www.ospreywatch.co.uk

FREE

I want to go here ☐

STROKE A SNAKE

...at Trotters World of Animals

Are you wary of wriggly reptiles? Scared of snakes? Then trot over to Trotters to conquer your fears.

Trotters World of Animals is a wildlife park with plenty of unusual species on display. They've got a swimming cat (the Asian fishing cat), the world's largest monkey species (a Mandrill) and the world's smallest otter (the Asian short-clawed otter).

Our favourite part of the farm is the Reptile Encounter. There you'll meet Beast, the resident boa constrictor, who likes nothing more than a cuddle with the visitors.

Sticker Scores

5	4	3
SNAKE CHARMER	PYTHON PAL	BOA BUDDY
2	1	
COBRA CONFIDANT	SNAKE HARMER	

Go on, give him a stroke! We're told he doesn't like to eat anything bigger than a rat, so you should be safe . . .

Make A Day Of It

 Watch the fantastic falconry displays at Trotters – vultures, owls and hawks circle above you, and a falcon dives at 100 miles per hour.

There are feeding displays throughout the day and you're encouraged to handle the animals. Enjoy the great play areas as well as tractor and pony rides.

Photo Op

Take a snap of you and Beast together and show it to your friends to freak them out!

Fascinating Facts

★ **Boa constrictors are one of the world's largest snakes, and can grow to be more than four metres long. That's as long as three nine year old kids lying end to end! They're not poisonous, but they are still lethal. (The boa constrictors, not the nine year old kids.)**

★ Boa constrictors kill by coiling their bodies around their prey to squish it to death. They usually eat birds, lizards, frogs and small mammals, but larger ones will munch on monkeys, pigs or deer.

★ **Up to 50,000 people are killed by snake bites every year. Venomous vipers and killer cobras are the biggest culprits. The boa constrictor, on the other hand, is not usually a harmer of humans.**

PLAN YOUR VISIT 9

Trotters World of Animals

Coalbeck Farm, Bassenthwaite, CA12 4RD

www.trottersworld.com

 01768 776239

Daily 10.00-17.30 (or dusk)

I want to go here

WATCH A PLAY

...at the Theatre by the Lake

There are loads of ways to add some drama to your trip to the Lake District. One way is to have a big family argument in the car. But we think a better way is to visit the Theatre by the Lake in Keswick.

The Theatre by the Lake is the home of Cumbria's leading professional theatre company. But the acting is not the only attraction – the theatre is set beside the shores of Derwent Water, and has dramatic views out onto the lake.

Sticker Scores

5 TERRIFIC THESPIAN

4 EXTRAORDINARY ENTERTAINER

3 AMATEUR ACTOR

2 POOR PLAYWRIGHT

1 USELESS UNDERSTUDY

Visit for a look around or book in advance to go to a performance. The programme includes plays and concerts for kids from time to time, so check online for details.

Make A Day Of It

🔑 Take one of the famous Keswick Launches on Derwent Water for a 50 minute round trip in a boat with several landing points. The Keswick Launch Company is a two minute walk away from the Theatre by the Lake.

🔑 If you don't fancy an organised cruise, then why not hire a rowing boat or a self-drive motor boat to explore the lake?

Did you hear about the actor who fell through the floor?

It was just a stage he was going through!

Fascinating Facts

★ The Theatre by the Lake started life in a box! Or, more specifically, as a travelling theatre called the Blue Box. For two decades it brought plays to people in a self-contained mobile trailer complete with a stage! The Blue Box parked in Keswick in 1976 and served as the town's theatre for twenty years until it was finally replaced by the new venue.

Photo Op
Find a good spot inside the theatre and pretend to be an actor. Get a snap of you striking a suitably dramatic pose.

PLAN YOUR VISIT 10

Theatre by the Lake
Lakeside, Keswick, CA12 5DJ
www.theatrebythelake.co.uk

📞 01768 774411

🕐 Theatre building open to public daily from 09.30, closed during performances

££ – £££

I want to go here ☐

PAT A ZEBROID

...at Eden Ostrich World

What do you get when you cross a zebra and a pony? No, this isn't the start of a bad joke. The surprising answer is that you get a real animal called a zebroid.

Eden Ostrich World is home to one of these rare little creatures, called Pozee Tinkerbell. Her mum is a Shetland pony and her dad is a zebra. The unlikely parents shared a paddock for a while and then amazed the world when they produced a foal.

There's plenty to do here besides patting Pozee. As the name suggests, this working farm has a flock of African black ostriches – you can see their eggs hatch in the summer. You'll also find meerkats, wallabies and rare breeds of cattle, sheep and pigs.

Sticker Scores

5 ZANY ZEBROID

4 OUTSTANDING OSTRICH

3 PECULIAR PONY

2 MERRY MEERKAT

1 RIDICULOUS RACOON

Best Of The Rest

🔑 Visit the adventure play areas where you can slide down a zip wire, attack an assault course and master a maze!

🔑 Watch Friesland sheep being milked at the farm (daily February to October).

🔑 If the weather is rubbish, you can hang out in the two-storey soft play area, complete with slides and a ball pool.

What do you call a three-legged donkey?

A wonkey!

Fascinating Facts

★ Different equine animals (including zebras, horses and donkeys) can mate together and produce crazy cross species (or hybrids). Examples include zorses, zonies and zedonks. Other hybrid animals do exist, such as ligers, tigons and wolphins (a very rare cross between a dolphin and a false killer whale).

★ Sadly, not all animals are named in this way. An elephant is not a cross between an elf and an ant, for example. And a leopard is definitely not a cross between a leprechaun and a shepherd.

★ Zebroids usually have some zebra stripes, but often not all over. Pozee Tinkerbell has some dark and light brown stripes on her legs and body.

PLAN YOUR VISIT 11

Eden Ostrich World

Langwathby Hall Farm, Langwathby, Penrith, CA10 1LW

www.ostrich-world.com

📞 01768 881771

🕐 Daily (summer) 10.00-17.00
Wed-Sun (out of season) 10.00-16.00

££

I want to go here ☐

FIND A STATELY HOME'S SECRET ROO

...at Dalemain House and Gardens

Being a Catholic priest in the 1500s wasn't easy. The religion was illegal, so if you were caught you were punished. And we're not talking about an hour on the naughty step. We're talking death by hanging. *Ouch*!

The owners of Dalemain House were clearly sympathetic with the Catholics, because they built a secret hiding place (known as a priest's hole) for persecuted priests. Once you've found it, see if you can spot another (even smaller) secret room – built into a staircase is the tiny window and door of Mrs Mouse's house.

After some indoor exploring, you can join the keeper in the gardens to feed wild birds and deer from your hands. Just don't try without him – it's dangerous unless you have expert assistance.

Sticker Scores

5 SECRET ROOM
4 LIVING ROOM
3 BATHROOM
2 BOX ROOM
1 NO ROOM

Best Of The Rest

🔑 Try the epic chocolate cake in the Medieval Tearoom. We reckon it's world-class!

🔑 Check out the museums in Dalemain's sixteenth-century barn. There's a Countryside Museum with loads of ancient farming equipment, and a Fell Pony Museum with a blacksmith's workshop.

Top Tip

Arrive first thing in the morning to take a guided tour of the house. The guides are good fun and will let you in on some of the house's other secrets!

Fascinating Facts

★ **Dalemain House has belonged to the same family since 1679 – that's *eleven* generations! Thankfully they've redecorated since they first moved in.**

★ Dalemain is in red squirrel country, and the owners are fans of these cute creatures. There's a squirrel in the family coat of arms, and you'll also find a picture of one in every room of the house! See if you can spot them all.

Butler – what's this fly doing in my soup?
Looks like backstroke to me, Sir!

PLAN YOUR VISIT 12

Dalemain House and Gardens
Dalemain, Penrith, CA11 0HB
www.dalemain.com

📞 **01768 486450**

🕐 House & gardens: Sun-Thu (summer) 10.30-16.00
Gardens: Sun-Thu (out of season) 11.00-16.00

£

I want to go here ☐

EXPLORE MEDIEVAL DUNGEONS

...at Carlisle Castle

Carlisle is near the Scottish border, which in the old days made it an ideal spot for scraps between the English and the Scots. And by scraps, we don't mean bits of food. We mean a big, bloody battle . . .

Carlisle Castle was first built in the 1100s, and part of the original construction (the keep) still survives. You can climb up the ancient stone stairways or, if you dare, descend into the dark dungeons!

Look out for the famous 'licking stones' during your visit. Prisoners were so thirsty that they licked the dungeon's stones for moisture. It didn't do them much good – they were usually executed anyway on nearby Gallows Hill. We'd rather lick a lolly!

Sticker Scores

5 — MILKSHAKE

4 — LEMONADE

3 — ORANGE JUICE

2 — ICE LOLLY

1 — LICKING STONE

Who is strong enough to move a castle?

A chess player!

Make A Day Of It

 Visit Tullie House Museum and Art Gallery in the centre of Carlisle. There you can fire a Roman weapon, climb a section of Hadrian's Wall and travel on an Edwardian train.

 Get up close to the Listening Wall at the Millennium Gallery, which links Tullie House to Carlisle Castle. You'll hear Carlisle people talking about stuff through small speakers in the wall.

 Steam across to Settle. The beautiful Carlisle-Settle railway is one of England's most famous rail journeys. Special steam trips are held every year on a chartered train and you need to book ahead. Check **www.uksteam.info** for details.

Fascinating Facts

⭐ Carlisle was the location for the first postbox on the British mainland. It was placed in Botchergate in Carlisle in 1853. The first postboxes were bronze, then green, and they only started being painted red in the 1870s. A replica of the original box stands outside the Tourist Information Centre in Carlisle – see if you can spot it!

Kite over Carlisle Castle

PLAN YOUR VISIT ⑬

Carlisle Castle
Castle Way, Carlisle, CA3 8UR
www.english-heritage.org.uk

 01228 591922

🕐 Daily 09.30-1700 (summer)
Daily 10.00-1600 (out of season)

£ 🎁

I want to go here ☐

WATCH A 3D FILM INSIDE A HILL

...at the Rheged Centre

The Rheged Centre is Europe's largest grass-covered building. But then maybe that's not too tricky – generally architects don't design something and then think: *Ooh, I know, let's cover it with grass.*

However, Rheged is different from most buildings. For a start, it has been built to look like a Lakeland hill, complete with limestone crags and waterfalls. And, more importantly, it's equipped with a massive 3D movie screen!

The 3D cinema is as tall as six double-decker buses, so you feel like you're in the centre of all the action.

Sticker Scores

⭐ **5** — HEAVENLY HILL

⭐ **4** — MASSIVE MOUND

⭐ **3** — FANCY FELL

⭐ **2** — PIFFLING PROMONTORY

⭐ **1** — OVER THE HILL

Sit back and watch dinosaurs fight around you, or let fish swim through your fingertips. Just don't try growing a garden on your roof when you get home!

Best Of The Rest

🔑 Go potty at Rheged's Create pottery workshop. You can paint your own designs on mugs, bowls, figures or money boxes, then take them home with you.

🔑 Roll around in the indoor soft play area which has a whole load of plastic balls.

🔑 Clamber around at Turrets and Tunnels, Rheged's outdoor activity zone. It's got a Roman fort, a giant slide and a cool climbing area.

> **Why did the skeleton go to the cinema by himself?**
> Because he *no body* to go with!

Fascinating Facts

⭐ Rheged was originally the name of the ancient kingdom of Cumbria which existed during the sixth century. At that time it was one of the most powerful parts of the land and covered most of North West England.

⭐ Covering buildings in grass is more common than you might think. For thousands of years people have used straw (a form of dried long grass) to make thatched roofs. Skilled thatchers can arrange the straw so that the roof lasts for up to 50 years before it needs to be replaced.

PLAN YOUR VISIT 14

Rheged Centre
Redhills, Penrith, CA11 0DQ
www.rheged.com

📞 01768 868000

🕐 Daily 10.00-17.30
Films hourly 11.00-16.00

££ (films)   £ (other activities)

I want to go here ☐

PLAY WITH 250 YEAR OLD TOYS

...at Wordsworth House and Gardens

How do you liven up a historical house when the famous person who lived there died a long time ago? The people who run Wordsworth House came up with a clever idea: put the people back in!

Don't worry though, you won't be meeting corpses. Instead the staff play the roles of the original inhabitants of Wordsworth House – the childhood home of William Wordsworth (see p62).

The house contains a working kitchen where you can help with the cooking and taste original recipes. The servants might ask you for a hand with the washing and cleaning, so watch out if you don't like housework! Alternatively, head to the children's bedroom to play with replica 250 year old toys such as skittles, dolls and jumping jacks.

Sticker Scores

5 SUPER SKITTLES

4 DELIGHTFUL DOLLS

3 JUMPING JACKS

2 PASSABLE PUPPET

1 WASHING UP

Make A Day Of It

🔑 Head to Harris Park for a nice stroll along the river and through woodland. There's a children's playground and lovely views over the historic town.

🔑 Follow the Cockermouth Town Trail. A series of small metal plaques lead you on a historical journey which includes a view of ancient Cockermouth Castle.

What should you call a bald teddy?

Fred bear!

Fascinating Facts

⭐ A jumping jack is a sort of cross between a puppet and a paper doll. A piece of string is tied to the legs and arms, so that when you pull it they move. It looks like the puppet is jumping – hence the name. Hundreds of years ago they were as exciting as a new Nintendo.

⭐ Cockermouth was devastated by floods in 2009. Water levels reached a terrifying 2.5 metres, leaving much of the town underwater and completely submerging the ground floors of lots of buildings. Many parts of Cumbria were hit hard by the floods, but Cockermouth suffered more than anywhere else. Wordsworth House has a flood trail which shows just how high the water reached.

PLAN YOUR VISIT 15

Wordsworth House and Gardens

Main Street, Cockermouth, CA13 9RX

www.nationaltrust.org.uk

📞 **01900 820884**

🕐 Sat-Wed (Mar-Oct) 11.00-17.00
Thu (Peak only) 11.00-17.00

I want to go here ☐

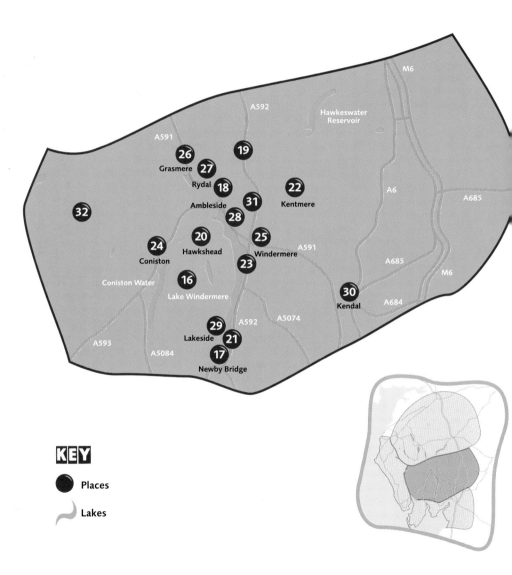

KEY

Places

Lakes

SOUTH LAKES

WEST COAST

SOUTH COAST

TOP FIVES

SWING FROM A TREE

...in Grizedale Forest

Feel like monkeying around? Fancy a gorilla thriller? Then you'll want to get yourself over to Go Ape in Grizedale Forest for some energetic outdoor activity!

Grizedale is the largest forest in the Lake District. It's also home to Go Ape, an awesome assault course high up in the tree tops. You climb ladders, hang onto Tarzan swings and slide down zip lines. At one point, you are nineteen metres above the ground. That's higher than eleven gorillas standing on each other's heads (and almost as scary)! We think *yew* will agree that it's *tree*-mendous!

Sticker Scores

⭐ 5 — **AMAZING APE**

⭐ 4 — **GIANT GORILLA**

⭐ 3 — **MEDIOCRE MONKEY**

⭐ 2 — **BUMBLING BABOON**

⭐ 1 — **COWARDLY CHIMP**

Best Of The Rest

If you haven't got a head for heights, then why not follow some of the marked walking trails through the forest? You can get maps from the visitor centre.

Hire a bike and explore the forest. There are five cycle trails with fantastic views of the fells (that's a Lakeland word for really large hills).

Visit one of the observation hides and spot forest wildlife. If you're really quiet, you might see squirrels, grouse, woodpeckers and even roe deer.

Why did the squirrel go nuts?
Because the monkey had gone bananas!

Fascinating Facts

Grizedale Forest is also an outdoor art museum. Artists have created all kinds of sculptures from natural materials like wood and stone. There are now around ninety works of art dotted through the forest for walkers and cyclists to discover. See how many you can find!

Top Tip
You have to be ten years old and taller than 1.4 metres to take part – so measure yourself before you book!

PLAN YOUR VISIT 16

Go Ape! Grizedale
Hawkshead, LA22 0QJ
www.goape.co.uk

 0845 643 9215

Daily except some Tuesdays (peak)
Opening selected days out of season
Opening hours vary

£££

I want to go here ☐

ROW A BOAT

...in Fell Foot Park

There are lots of spots to go for a row in the Lake District. After all, it's not like they're short of water! Our favourite is Fell Foot Park – and we reckon it will *float your boat* too!

Perched at the southern end of Lake Windermere, Fell Foot Park was originally the gardens of a grand Victorian mansion house. The house was demolished back in 1907 but the old boathouse building remains and is now a tea room. You can hire boats from there and have a go at rowing over to Lakeside and back. The huge lawns next to the lake are great for picnics and there's a top adventure playground too.

Sticker Scores

5 — FLEET FOOTED
4 — NEW SHOES
3 — FOOTLOOSE

2 — POOR PAWS
1 — FLAT FOOTED

Knock knock.
Who's there?
Rhoda.
Rhoda Who?
Rho-Rho-Rho-da boat gently down the stream!

Make A Day Of It

 Across the road from Fell Foot Park you'll see a signpost for Gummers How car park. Gummers How is the highest viewpoint at the southern end of Lake Windermere and it's an easy, fun climb.

 A short drive away is Sizergh Castle. This medieval castle has a great treasure hunt around its beautiful gardens.

 Local organic farm Low Sizergh Barn has a lovely two mile farm trail. Spot chickens, cattle and sheep as well as ancient hedges and woodland when you follow the marked path.

Fascinating Facts

★ **The Fell Foot estate was originally home to a family called the Robinsons. Two of the last brothers to live there sound more like pirates than estate owners: Terrible Dick was known for being foul-mouthed, and Black Jack got his name because he had a long black beard. *Arrrrr!***

★ Fell Foot is not the only location to have an association with feet. For example, Plumpton Foot, North Shoebury and Sockburn are all real UK place names!

Top Tip

Take an anorak along even if it's not raining to stop yourself from getting soaked by the splashing oars.

PLAN YOUR VISIT 17

Fell Foot Park

Newby Bridge, Ulverston, LA12 8NN

www.nationaltrust.org.uk

📞 01539 531273

🕐 Boats for hire daily (summer) 11.00-16.00

£ - ££

I want to go here ☐

...at Bridge House

How big do you think a house needs to be to fit a family of eight? Well, Bridge House only has two tiny rooms yet it was home to Mr and Mrs Rigg and their *six* children!

Bridge House is a minuscule stone building that used to be an apple store. It's the smallest house in Cumbria, and is strangely arranged over two floors. And, as if that wasn't silly enough, it's also perched on top of a tiny bridge!

The building is now a National Trust shop, so anyone can go in. Step inside the tiny rooms and imagine what the conditions must have been like for the Riggs. We just hope they all got along well together . . .

Sticker Scores

5 HUMUNGOUS HOUSE

4 ROOMY RESIDENCE

3 DECENT DWELLING

2 COMPACT COTTAGE

1 DOLL'S HOUSE

Make A Day Of It

🔑 If you're into football, don't miss nearby attraction The Homes of Football, a huge gallery of football photography recording games, fans and stadiums from around the world.

🔑 For a bit of peace and quiet, explore Borrans Park down by the lake. It's the perfect place for picnicking and paddling. Beside the park is the site of the Roman fort Galava.

🔑 Take a short walk from behind the Salutation Hotel to visit Stock Ghyll Force, a beautiful waterfall with a 23 metre drop.

Fascinating Facts

⭐ **The biggest house in the world is Windsor Castle near London, where the Queen lives. It covers around 45,000 square metres and contains 1,000 rooms. You could fit seven football pitches inside and still have space for a playroom and paddling pool! There are bigger buildings in the world, but this is thought to be the biggest that is someone's home.**

⭐ A man from America called Jay Shafer has designed a house that covers just six square metres. That means it's about as wide as an adult, and as long as two eleven year olds. We've seen bigger garden sheds before!

Doctor, doctor, I think I'm a bridge? Why, what's come over you!

PLAN YOUR VISIT 18

Bridge House
Rydal Road, Ambleside, LA22 9AN
www.visitcumbria.com

📞 01539 432617

🕐 Daily (summer) 10.00–17.00

FREE

I want to go here ☐

STRUGGLE UP THE STRUGGLE

...at The Struggle

The Struggle sounds like the name of a piece of depressing modern art, but it is in fact an extremely steep road. It also has some of the most dramatic views in the Lake District.

The Struggle leads from the village of Ambleside to the top of the Kirkstone Pass. The road zigzags up over 400 metres in just over three miles at a gradient of 25% – that's as steep as an intermediate ski slope!

In the old days, horses found The Struggle so difficult that passengers would often have to get out of carriages and climb the hill on foot. Nowadays it's a tough climb even for some cars. So you'd better hope you don't break down!

Sticker Scores

5 SUPER STRUGGLER

4 TERRIFIC TOILER

3 STANDARD STRIVER

2 LOUSY LABOURER

1 GIVEN UP

Make A Day Of It

🔑 Look out for the Kirk Stone, a large stone landmark at the side of the road. The word kirk comes from the Norse word for church. From some views the stone is said to look like a church steeple.

🔑 Stop off at the 500 year-old Kirkstone Pass Inn for a bite to eat. It's the third highest pub in the country, and offers a friendly welcome and crackling log fires.

Photo Op
Stop at a safe place along the road and get a snap of you struggling up The Struggle. Make the most pained expression you can!

Fascinating Facts

⭐ **Ghosts are said to haunt the isolated Kirkstone Pass. One of the most famous is a young lady called Ruth Ray who set off with her baby to visit her father. A blizzard came down and she did not return. In the morning she was found frozen to death, but her baby, whom she had wrapped in her shawl, miraculously survived. She supposedly haunts the Pass, warning travellers to beware of the fast-changing weather.**

What did the cart driver say to his horse?

Why the long face?

PLAN YOUR VISIT 19
The Struggle
Kirkstone Pass (A592), Ambleside, LA22
www.visitcumbria.com

FREE

I want to go here ☐

...at Hawkshead Grammar School

If you think *your* school day is hard, then be glad you didn't live in the eighteenth century! You'd have had to cope with a six o'clock start in summer (with a lie-in until seven in winter) . . . and if that wasn't bad enough, all your lessons would be in Latin or ancient Greek!

This was the typical life of an eighteenth-century schoolboy at Hawkshead Grammar School. The school closed in the early 1900s, and it's now a museum with excellent guided tours. The classroom looks just as it would have done 200 years ago – there are no white boards or computers here. And that's not all that's changed: back then, schoolboys were allowed to drink beer and smoke cigarettes at school!

Sticker Scores

5 STAR SCHOOLBOY

4 SUPER STUDENT

3 BRAINY BOOKWORM

2 LAZY LEARNER

1 SCHOOLBOY ERROR

Make A Day Of It

🔑 Explore the ancient village of Hawkshead with its old houses, squares and higgledy-piggledy streets. The Beatrix Potter Gallery in the centre is full of original drawings from her books.

🔑 Visit nearby Hill Top Farm, which was Beatrix Potter's home when she created Tom Kitten, Samuel Whiskers and Jemima Puddleduck. The house remains exactly as it was when Beatrix lived there.

🔑 Walk from Hawkshead up to Tarn Hows. A tarn is a local word for a small lake, and Tarn Hows is one of the most beautiful spots in the Lake District.

Fascinating Facts

⭐ In the museum you will find the school's original silver wax seal. The picture on the seal is the school-master with a birch in his hand. The birch is a long wooden rod that was used to thwack badly behaved children! Clearly the school was proud of its tough discipline . . .

⭐ William Wordsworth was the most famous pupil to pass through the school gates. See if you can spot where the young poet carved his name in one of the desks.

> Did you hear about the cross-eyed teacher?
> He couldn't control his pupils!

PLAN YOUR VISIT 20

Hawkshead Grammar School
Hawkshead, LA22 0NT
www.hawksheadgrammar.org.uk

📞 01539 436735

🕐 Mon-Sat (summer) 10.00-12.30
& 13.30-17.00
Sun (summer) 13.00-17.00

£

I want to go here ☐

WALK UNDER A LAKE

...at the Lakes Aquarium

Walking underwater is not normally something we'd recommend. It's wetter than the average pavement, and there's more chance of drowning. But you can do it in the Lakes Aquarium without worrying . . .

The Lakes Aquarium is full of lake-dwelling animals from all over the world. There are cheeky otters, eyeless Mexican fish, and sharks from nearby Morecambe Bay. The star attraction is an incredible underwater tunnel which recreates the murky depths of Lake Windermere. As you walk through you are surrounded by fish such as carp and brown trout. You can even see ducks' feet paddling away above your head!

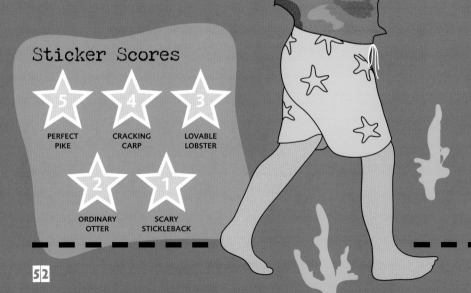

Sticker Scores

5 PERFECT PIKE

4 CRACKING CARP

3 LOVABLE LOBSTER

2 ORDINARY OTTER

1 SCARY STICKLEBACK

Make A Day Of It

🔑 Catch a steam train on the Lakeside and Haverthwaite Railway. The railway line is 140 years old, and runs along a four mile stretch of the Backbarrow Gorge. Lakeside station is next to the aquarium.

🔑 Continue your journey with a cruise on Lake Windermere (see p66). The steam railway train timetable is organised to tie in with the boats.

> Did you hear about the otter that lived on the moon?
>
> They say he came from *otter*-space!

Fascinating Facts

⭐ **Otters are extremely intelligent. They are among the few animals who can use tools – for example they smash rocks onto shells to crack them open. They're also able to hold their breath for up to eight minutes underwater and have a special skin on their ears and nose which keeps them watertight. Think of it as nature's own otter goggles!**

Top Tip

Time your aquarium visit to coincide with the otters being fed. This happens twice a day – contact the aquarium before you travel to check the otters' meal times.

PLAN YOUR VISIT 21

Lakes Aquarium

Lakeside, Newby Bridge, LA12 8AS

www.lakesaquarium.co.uk

📞 01539 530153

🕐 Daily (summer) 09.00-18.00
Daily (out of season) 09.00-17.00

££

I want to go here ☐

POST A LETTER FROM POSTMAN PAT

...in Kentmere

If you've ever watched *Postman Pat*, you'll know he lives in the Greendale Valley. What you may not know is that Greendale is based on a real place called Kentmere.

The *Postman Pat* stories were written by John Cunliffe, who lived near Kentmere. If you visit, you can see that it looks just like the valley in the stories. You can explore the paths that Pat and Jess would have driven along in their red van. Hire a bike from nearby Staveley, or take a walk led by a National Park guide. Alternatively, if you're feeling lazy, you can take a little bus called the Kentmere Rambler.

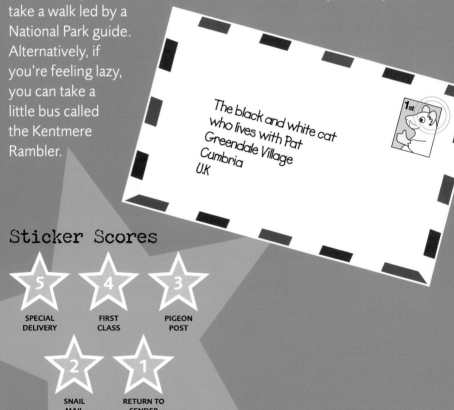

The black and white cat who lives with Pat
Greendale Village
Cumbria
U.K

1st

Sticker Scores

5 — SPECIAL DELIVERY

4 — FIRST CLASS

3 — PIGEON POST

2 — SNAIL MAIL

1 — RETURN TO SENDER

ALLEY

Best Of The Rest

🔑 See old mill buildings and machinery used to manufacture cotton at Staveley Mill Yard. Wilf's Café is a great place for a bite to eat too.

🔑 If you don't want to take a guided walk, go on a walking trail instead. Follow the River Kent from Staveley to Kentmere village. From Kentmere Hall there are lots of walking trails where you can spot grouse, rabbits and even wild ponies.

What do you get if you cross a tiger with a guard dog?

A terrified postman!

Fascinating Facts

★ The River Kent is one of the fastest flowing in England. Local people have used it to power mills, which grind grain, for hundreds of years.

★ The valley once had a huge lake at the bottom. In 1840 it was drained, like a giant bathtub, to make way for farmland.

★ The Royal Mail has around 80,000 postmen (and postwomen!) working for it across a network of 12,000 post offices. So Pat is a just a small piece of the postal picture.

Top Tip

Send someone a postcard from Staveley Post Office. Sign it as Postman Pat!

PLAN YOUR VISIT 22

Kentmere
Near Kendal, Cumbria
www.golakes.co.uk

FREE

I want to go here ☐

55

CUDDLE UP TO PETER RABBIT

...at the World of Beatrix Potter

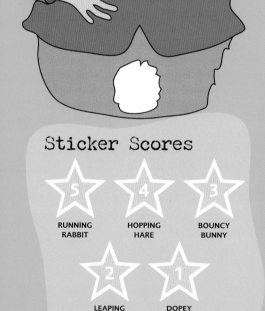

Hop, skip and jump along to the World of Beatrix Potter, an indoor attraction where you'll catch Peter Rabbit stealing vegetables from Mr McGregor's garden.

Beatrix wrote her first book, *The Tale of Peter Rabbit*, more than 100 years ago. She became one of the best-known and most-loved children's authors. Today her tales are brought to life in an indoor re-creation of the Lakeland countryside with animals that move, pour tea, fish, stretch and wiggle. You can visit Mrs Tiggy-Winkle ironing in her kitchen and drop in on Jemima Puddleduck.

You can even sniff the smells of the countryside – although you might prefer to hold your nose!

Sticker Scores

5	4	3
RUNNING RABBIT	HOPPING HARE	BOUNCY BUNNY

2	1
LEAPING LEVERET	DOPEY DOE

Best Of The Rest

🔑 The Peter Rabbit garden is full of the gooseberry bushes and carrots that Peter couldn't resist!

🔑 If you want to try vegetables from the garden, the café has a tasty kids' menu using home-made ingredients, as well as colouring sheets and games.

Photo Op
The World of Beatrix Potter has a pretty impressive photo booth which lets you include yourself in photographs with Peter, Jemima and Mrs Tiggy-Winkle!

Fascinating Facts

⭐ Beatrix Potter started drawing her own pet rabbit – who really was called Peter – when she was a very little girl. She and her brother had lots of pets, including a green frog, two lizards, some water newts, a ring snake and a tortoise as well as Peter the Rabbit. Almost all of the famous characters in her books are based on her real pets!

⭐ The Peter Rabbit series has sold more than 151 million copies worldwide, and has been translated into 35 different languages!

How do you know carrots are good for your eyes? Because you never see rabbits wearing glasses!

PLAN YOUR VISIT 23

The World of Beatrix Potter Attraction
Bowness-on-Windermere, LA23 3BX
www.hop-skip-jump.com

📞 01539 488444

🕐 Daily (summer) 10.00-17.30
Daily (out of season) 10.00-16.30

££

I want to go here ☐

GO ON A GONDOLA

...on Coniston Water

If you thought the only place you could go on a gondola ride was in Venice, think again. On Coniston Water, you can take a trip on *Gondola*, a rebuilt Victorian steam yacht!

Gondola is long and thin with a high prow (that's the official boaty name for the front end). In other words, she's a bit like the gondola boats in Venice, but much larger, and powered by steam instead of arm muscle! *Gondola* carried tourists from 1860 until 1963, when huge storms washed her ashore. After that she lay shipwrecked until she was restored by the National Trust. Now you can once again take *Gondola* on Coniston. Just don't expect the captain to wear a striped T-shirt and sing to you in Italian.

Sticker Scores

5 GREAT GONDOLIER

4 FANTASTIC FERRYMAN

3 ORDINARY OARSMAN

2 HOPELESS HELMSMAN

1 ROTTEN ROWER

Best Of The Rest

🔑 Trek to the top of The Old Man of Coniston. Don't worry though, you won't be climbing up a wrinkly man who looks like your grandad – it's the name of an 800 metre high mountain. Allow four hours for the round trip.

🔑 Spot the remains of abandoned copper mines and quarries in Coppermines Valley.

🔑 If *Gondola* isn't running, you can still take a trip on the Coniston Launch, which is the other cruise service on the lake.

What did the sea say to the boat?
Nothing, it just waved!

Fascinating Facts

⭐ In 1967 a daredevil motorboat racer called Donald Campbell tried to break his own world water speed record on Coniston. His jet-powered boat *Bluebird* reached 320 miles per hour then flipped over. Campbell was killed and his teddy-bear mascot Mr Whoppit was found floating among the wreckage of the boat. He (Campbell, not Mr Whoppit) is now buried in Coniston churchyard.

⭐ Arthur Ransome based his book *Swallows and Amazons* on his childhood adventures on Coniston Water. Peel Island at the southern end of the lake gave him the idea for Wildcat Island in the book. And *Gondola* originally gave him the idea for Captain Flint's houseboat!

PLAN YOUR VISIT 24

Coniston Pier
Coniston, LA21 8AN
www.nationaltrust.org.uk

📞 01539 441288

🕐 Daily (summer) 10.30-16.15
Sailings are weather permitting – call ahead to check

££   NT

I want to go here ☐

CLIMB UP A FELL

...at Orrest Head

A fell is a local word for a large hill. When in the Lake District it would be rude not to climb at least one. So why not start with one of the most famous fell walks and climb Orrest Head?

Orrest Head has one of the best views in the Lake District. On a clear day, from the top you can see Windermere, Morecambe Bay, central Lakeland and even the Yorkshire Dales. That's a lot of view from one spot!

It takes about twenty minutes to walk to the top from Windermere Station.

On your way you'll pass through the beautiful Elleray Wood, where you'll find a blacksmith's workshop. There are also benches along the route if you need a breather.

Sticker Scores

5 AWESOME ADVENTURER

4 FEARLESS FELLWALKER

3 HEROIC HIKER

2 TOILING TREKKER

1 FELL OVER

Best Of The Rest

🔑 Take the train from Oxenholme to Windermere Station at the bottom of Orrest Head. The journey through the River Kent valley is a great way to arrive at Orrest Head!

🔑 Windermere Tourist Office is a good place to get your bearings – they can show you the starting point for the Orrest Head walk.

🔑 Beside Windermere station there's a huge kitchen shop called Lakeland with a great café upstairs. Let the grown-ups browse for pots and pans and they might buy you a hot chocolate to thank you for waiting patiently!

Fascinating Facts

⭐ **Alfred Wainwright, a famous author of guide books for grown-ups, walked up Orrest Head in 1930. He liked the view so much that he moved to the Lake District!**

⭐ Wainwright is particularly well known for his Lake District fell-walking guides. They describe walks up 214 fells, which these days are commonly known as the Wainwrights.

⭐ **The youngest person to scale all the Wainwright peaks was just *five years old* at the time! So you have no excuse not to walk up at least one of them . . .**

Why doesn't a fell get cold in the winter? It has a snow cap!

PLAN YOUR VISIT 25
Orrest Head
Windermere, LA23
www.english-lakes.com

FREE

I want to go here ☐

61

VISIT A POET'S GRAVE

...at St Oswald's Church

Going to a grave may not sound like a cheerful way to spend a day, but the tombstone of William Wordsworth in St Oswald's Church is a pretty and peaceful spot. It sits under yew trees planted by Wordsworth himself.

Wordsworth lived near St Oswald's church in Dove Cottage, on the outskirts of Grasmere village, from 1799 to 1808. During this period he wrote much of his poetry, including the famous 'Daffodils' poem, which starts with the words 'I wandered lonely as a cloud'. Presumably he was talking about just one cloud on an otherwise sunny day.

Sticker Scores

5 POET LAUREATE

4 BRILLIANT BARD

3 SIMPLE SCRIBBLER

2 AWFUL AUTHOR

1 ROTTEN RHYMER

In our experience clouds in the Lake District usually have quite a few other clouds nearby to keep them company!

Best Of The Rest

Visit Wordsworth's home at Dove Cottage, which is now the Wordsworth Museum and Art Gallery. It contains William's old ice skates – back then Grasmere lake froze over in winter!

Follow the wonderful smell to Sarah Nelson's, Grasmere's famous Gingerbread Shop, just next to the church.

Take a picnic down to Grasmere lake where you can hire rowing boats and kayaks.

Visit the Storytellers' Garden in the village centre where a well-known storyteller called Taffy Thomas will entertain you.

Fascinating Facts

★ Wordsworth was made Poet Laureate when he was 73 – the oldest Poet Laureate ever. The position is appointed by the Government and the holder is expected to write poems for important state occasions. Wordsworth is the only Poet Laureate who failed to produce a single official poem in his time in the post!

★ Nowadays there is also a Children's Laureate. The position is awarded to a writer or illustrator of children's books. Michael Rosen and Jacqueline Wilson are both former Children's Laureates.

★ A new position of Laureate For Storytelling was created in 2009 and the first award went to . . . Taffy Thomas!

PLAN YOUR VISIT 26

St Oswald's Church

Grasmere, LA22 9SW

FREE

Why are poets always so poor?
Because rhyme doesn't pay!

I want to go here ☐

63

WALK ALL THE WAY AROUND A LAK[E]

...at Rydal Water

Unlike most Lake District lakes, Rydal is easy to walk around. Just don't try taking a short cut – you'll get wet!

Rydal Water is the second smallest lake in the Lake District and you should be able to stroll around it in under an hour. There are lots of different routes so it's a good idea to take a map. We suggest you start your walk at White Moss Common. Cross the footbridge over the River Rothay, then take the lower path along the edge of the lake.

Sticker Scores

5 — **BRILLIANT BACKPACKER**

4 — **SUPER STROLLER**

3 — **WONDERFUL WAYFARER**

2 — **PATHETIC PEDESTRIAN**

1 — **UNDER WATER**

A steep stony trail leads from here up to Rydal Cave, a spooky, disused slate quarry. Head back from there towards the main road. *Water* fun way to spend a day!

Make A Day Of It

 Visit Rydal Mount and Dora's Field, to the east of the lake. Rydal Mount was home to the Wordsworth family for 46 years. When Wordsworth's daughter Dora died, he and his family filled the field next door to their home with hundreds of daffodils in her memory, and it has been named after her ever since.

 It may sound spooky, but The Coffin Trail, which starts behind Rydal Mount, is a beautiful walk back towards Grasmere. In medieval times, coffin bearers would use the route to carry bodies from Rydal to Grasmere.

What's a toad's favourite ballet?

Swamp Lake!

Fascinating Facts

★ Rydal is a glacial lake – which means it was created by a melting glacier. As the glaciers retreated at the end of the Ice Age, they left behind lakes that often had drumlins (hills) in the middle. Rydal Water's drumlin is a small wooded island called Heron Island.

★ The lake contains enough water to fill 80 million bath tubs (but has fewer rubber ducks in it)!

Top Tip

At the western edge of the lake, keep your eyes open for a rock known as Wordsworth's Seat. This was one of the poet's favourite places.

PLAN YOUR VISIT 27

Rydal Water
Rydal Village, Cumbria
www.visitcumbria.com

FREE NT

I want to go here ☐

CRUISE ON ENGLAND'S LARGEST LAK

...at Lake Windermere

Lake Windermere is so big that it actually has its own tide! It is the largest natural lake in England and makes the other ones in the Lake District seem like ponds in comparison.

You can explore the lake by catching one of the boats run by Windermere Lake Cruises. At ten and a half miles long and one mile wide, the lake is ideal for a leisurely cruise. Along the way you'll see isolated islands, thick forests, bustling boatyards and fantastic fells.

Start your journey at Bowness, Lakeside or Ambleside.

Sticker Scores

5 LARGE LAKE	4 TERRIFIC TARN	3 MIDDLING MOAT
2 PIDDLING POND	1 PATHETIC PUDDLE	

You'll be able to choose anything from a quick 45 minute island cruise to a Freedom of the Lake pass for serious Windermere explorers.

Make A Day Of It

🔑 Some cruises stop at the Brockhole Lake District Visitor Centre. Here you can fly over the Lake District on a magic carpet, or play on the awesome adventure playground!

🔑 At the Lakeside stop, you can visit the Aquarium of the Lakes (see p52) and take a train ride on the Lakeside and Haverthwaite Railway (see p53).

🔑 Buy a bag of duck food from one of the ice-cream vans or shops near Bowness Pier. Use it to feed the ducks, swans, doves, geese and gulls that will flock around you when they spot it!

Fascinating Facts

⭐ **Over 1,000 years ago, a vain Viking called Vinand decided to name the large lake he discovered after . . . himself! Over time Vinand's Mere (an old word for lake) became better known as Windermere.**

⭐ Confusingly, the village of Windermere is actually a mile away from the lake. Windermere was originally called Birthwaite, but in 1847 the name was changed to make it a more attractive tourist destination. (Clearly this worked!) Bowness-on-Windermere is nearer the lake – and that's where the cruises depart from.

> What time does a duck wake up?
> At the quack of dawn!

PLAN YOUR VISIT 28

Windermere Lake Cruises

Bowness Pier, Bowness-on-Windermere, LA23 3HQ

www.windermere-lakecruises.co.uk

📞 01539 443360

🕐 Daily (summer) 09.30-18.00
Daily (out of season) 10.00-16.00

££

I want to go here ☐

...at Stott Park Bobbin Mill

Do you get annoyed when you're asked to help with the housework? Well, be glad you were not born in the 1800s. Back then, poor children had to work all day in mills and factories . . .

At Stott Park Bobbin Mill, over 250 men and boys worked long hours in horrible conditions. Boys were particularly useful – their small hands and bodies meant they could squeeze in between machinery more easily than grown-ups. It was very dangerous work and many of them were injured or even killed. Today it's one of the last mills in England. But don't worry about being offered a job – they've stopped employing children now. Phew!

Sticker Scores

5 — MILL-IONAIRE

4 — MILL OWNER

3 — MILL MANAGER

2 — MILL WORKER

1 — RUN OF THE MILL

WORK IN MILLS

Best Of The Rest

🔑 Go at the right time of day and you can take a guided tour of the mill and find out how the 200 year old machinery works.

🔑 See the steam-powered water wheel that drives the machinery. It only runs on certain days, so check beforehand if you want to see it in action.

🔑 Walk through the woods from the mill to High Dam reservoir, which powers the water wheel.

> What do you call an army of bobbin-makers?
> The mill-itary!

Fascinating Facts

⭐ The mill was used to produce bobbins. Bobbins are the things that thread (like cotton or wool) is wound around to store it and keep it tangle-free. They're needed for making all woven cloth.

⭐ The mill was built in 1835 and at one time was producing over a quarter of a million cotton bobbins per week for the textile industry in Lancashire! When plastic bobbins replaced traditional wooden ones the mill went out of business, and so it became a demonstration mill.

⭐ Some of the boys at the mill were orphans who came from local workhouses. They had no pay or education. All they were given was a roof over their heads and two meals a day.

PLAN YOUR VISIT 29

Stott Park Bobbin Mill

Finsthwaite, LA12 8AX

www.english-heritage.org.uk

📞 01539 531087

🕐 Mon-Fri (summer) 11.00-17.00

I want to go here ☐

TRAVEL BACK IN TIME

...at The Museum of Lakeland Life

While the Museum of Lakeland Life doesn't strictly speaking have a time machine, it does have the next best thing.

The museum contains realistic re-creations of old rooms and shops that transport you back in time (sort of) to see what Cumbria used to look like. At the centre is a traditional street, where you can peer into an old-fashioned pharmacy and look into a toy shop.

We particularly like the replica Lakeland farmhouse. In the parlour you'll find a working gramophone – a sort of record player that people used to listen to music in the days before iPods. There's also a kitchen full of traditional utensils and recipes. Once you've visited, you'll see why we've made a meal out of it!

Sticker Scores

5 LAKELAND LIFE

4 VICTORIAN VALUES

3 GEORGIAN GAMES

2 EDWARDIAN UTENSILS

1 GET A LIFE

Make A Day Of It

🔑 Look for paintings of local landscapes in the Abbot Hall Gallery, which is in the same building as the museum. See how many you can find of places you have visited!

🔑 Head to the Kendal Museum to see a dinosaur footprint, try on Roman sandals and do a coin rubbing.

🔑 Visit the Quaker Tapestry. It's a huge piece of woven art that tells the story of the Quakers. Quakers, by the way, are *not* wobbling, scared people – they're a Christian religious group.

🔑 Taste some Kendal Mint Cake – it's the town's most famous export!

Fascinating Facts

⭐ Kendal Mint Cake is basically a bar of sugar, which is sometimes coated in chocolate. It's stuffed with so much energy that mountaineers are particularly fond of it. Sir Edmund Hillary – the first man to climb Mount Everest – took some with him on his journey. The sugary stuff is also given to the Irish army in their emergency ration pack!

What old-fashioned gadget corrects your punctuation as you speak?

A *grammar*-phone!

PLAN YOUR VISIT 30

Museum of Lakeland Life
Abbot Hall, Kendal, LA9 5AL
www.lakelandmuseum.org.uk

📞 01539 722464

🕐 Mon-Sat (summer) 10.30-17.00
Mon-Sat (out of season) 10.30-16.00

I want to go here ☐

MEET A YEOMAN FARMER

...at Townend

Troutbeck village contains the home of a yeoman farmer. A yeoman was farmer who owned his own land. They should not be confused with farmers from Yemen, a country in the Middle East with lots of oil and fish.

Townend is a traditional farmhouse that was built in 1626 for a yeoman sheep farmer called George Browne. His family lived in it for several hundred years and very little has been changed since.

You can explore the house and, at certain times, meet an actor playing one of the Browne family. In full Victorian dress, he will tell you all about life at Townend as a yeoman farmer. He will *not* tell you anything about life in Yemen . . .

Sticker Scores

5 YEOMAN	4 ROMAN	3 SNOWMAN
	2 LEMON	1 YEMEN

Make A Day Of It

 Step back in time at Troutbeck, a nearby village where nearly all the houses are more than 100 years old and twelve of them are more than 400 years old!

 Grab a bite to eat at The Queen's Head – a 400 year old coaching inn. There's a great kids' menu, and while you eat you can stare at the bar, which is made out of an old four poster bed!

How did farmers used to greet each other?
Yo, man!

Fascinating Facts

⭐ **The yeoman was a respected and hard-working farmer in English society. While he wasn't quite important enough to be considered a member of the gentry (posh people whose families owned big estates) he did own his own land and had some social status.**

⭐ The Republic of Yemen borders Oman and Saudi Arabia. It has around 24 million people, and much of the country is covered in sand. While there is some farming in the centre and west of the country, it still has nothing to do with yeomen.

PLAN YOUR VISIT 31

Townend

Troutbeck Village, Near Windermere, LA23 1LB

www.nationaltrust.org.uk

📞 **01539 432628**

🕐 **Wed-Sun: tours on the hour 11.00-13.00 (Mar-Oct)**
Wed-Sun: unguided access 13.00-17.00 (Mar-Oct)

£ ☂ NT

I want to go here ☐

PRETEND TO BE A ROMAN SOLDIER

...at Hardknott Roman Fort

The Romans seemed to get everywhere while they built the Roman Empire, and that included the Lake District. They weren't here to see the sights though. They were here to conquer (as in take over, not play with horse chestnuts).

The Romans built forts, roads, houses and even a navy base in the Lake District. Hardknott Fort is one of their constructions, and a great place to imagine what it was like to be a soldier. It's high up on a hill, so it must have been very lonely and frequently freezing cold – particularly when wearing a toga! Today you can still see the remains of the fort walls, the commander's house, the food stores and the Bath House where chilly soldiers could warm up.

Sticker Scores

5 MIGHTY EMPEROR

4 MASTERFUL COMMANDER

3 POWERFUL CENTURION

2 DUTIFUL SOLDIER

1 SORRY SLAVE

Best Of The Rest

Glannaventra is a Roman fort built on the cliffs above Ravenglass. It was home to 1,000 Roman soldiers. At two metres high they are the tallest Roman remains in the country.

The fort at Birdoswald has a good visitor centre that shows how it would have looked in Roman times.

Top Tip

Take a picnic with you and enjoy lunch looking out over the valley. We suggest you don't pack any stuffed dormice!

How was the Roman Empire cut in half?

With a pair of Caesars!

Fascinating Facts

⭐ Probably the most famous Roman fortification in England is Hadrian's Wall. The Emperor Hadrian ordered a wall to be built which stretched from coast to coast across the north of England. It's over 73 miles long, and much of it still exists today. Hadrian's Wall was built to protect the English from the hairy, scary tribes on the other side (the Scottish!) who had an annoying habit of stealing their cattle.

⭐ Romans liked their food. Although soldiers at a fort such as Hardknott would eat very basic rations, more wealthy Romans would eat peacocks' tongues, stuffed dormice and even ostrich brains!

PLAN YOUR VISIT 32

Hardknott Roman Fort

Hardknott Pass, Eskdale, Cumbria

www.english-heritage.org.uk

FREE

I want to go here ☐

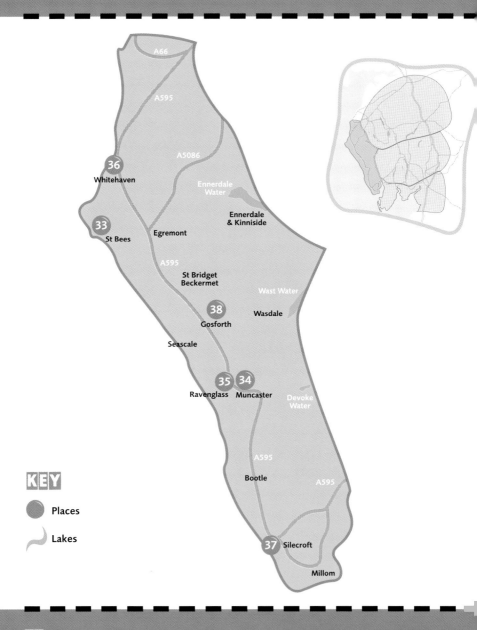

KEY

● Places

〰 Lakes

GO BEACHCOMBING FOR GEMS

...at St Bees Head

The beach at St Bees is a terrific place to go treasure hunting. You might not get rich, but you could find some great gemstones. Just watch out for jellyfish as you potter round the rock pools!

St Bees Head is a coastal nature reserve. It's particularly popular with birdwatchers who come to spot rare species like the black guillemot, which doesn't breed anywhere else in England. The shingle beach is also great for gemstone hunting. You'll find semi-precious stones like striped agate and bright-red jasper lying around on the beach. There's even the odd fish skeleton! They make great presents (the gemstones, not the dead fish).

Sticker Scores

5 MILLION DOLLAR DIAMOND

4 EXPENSIVE EMERALD

3 JOLLY JASPER

2 ATTRACTIVE AGATE

1 PATHETIC PEBBLE

Best Of The Rest

 At low tide, you can see 400 year old graffiti! Boys from the nearby boarding school, St Bees, used to carve words into the sandstone rocks on the beach.

 At the nearby St Bees Priory you can find the remains of a medieval knight known as St Bees Man. His coffin was dug up in 1981, and despite being dead for 600 years he still had perfectly preserved hair, neat nails and even food in his stomach!

Which bees are the cleverest?

Spelling bees!

Fascinating Facts

★ St Bees is named after an Irish Princess, St Bega. Legend has it that on Midsummer's Eve she asked the local lord for land to build a priory (a religious building). Laughing, he promised her as much ground as was covered by snow the following morning. The next day dawned – with three square miles of land deep in snow! So she got her building, and St Bees Priory has been there ever since.

Top Tip

Take your binoculars to St Bees Head for some birdwatching. See if you can tick off razorbills, kittiwakes, gulls, gannets and skuas. There are information points along the headland to help you spot the birds.

PLAN YOUR VISIT 33

St Bees Head
St Bees, CA27
www.visitcumbria.com

FREE

I want to go here ☐

GET SPOOKED

...at Muncaster Castle

Many houses in Britain are said to be haunted, but what causes these tales of the unexplained? At Muncaster, the owners tried to find out by letting a team of scientists come and investigate!

Muncaster Castle claims to be one of the most haunted castles in Britain. Researchers from Birmingham University suggested that the strange magnetic fields surrounding the castle may cause people to imagine the spooky stories. Or perhaps the stories come from the ghastly behaviour of real ghosts!

Take an audio tour, or play on the interactive computers in the old dairy to hear tales of Tom Fool, the castle's most famous ghost. He was the court jester at Muncaster in the 1500s, and supposedly still causes mischief today.

Sticker Scores

5 FANTASTIC PHANTOM

4 GLORIOUS GHOST

3 GLOOMY GHOUL

2 SURLY SPECTRE

1 SHEET OVER HEAD

Best Of The Rest

🔑 Pretend to be a vole in the castle's Meadowvole Maze. Imagine you are 6.5 centimetres tall and everything else is very, very big!

🔑 Visit the World Owl Centre, which is also part of the castle. Muncaster has one of the best owl collections in the world – from European eagle owls to pygmy owls. Think Hogwarts but without the magic . . .

🔑 Watch herons being fed at Heron Happy Hour! It takes place daily at 15.30.

🔑 Alternatively, why not just wander around the pretty gardens?

Fascinating Facts

⭐ Tom Fool the jester had a strange sense of humour. He would apparently sit outside the doors of the castle under a chestnut tree. If he didn't like the look of travellers who asked the way, he would direct them into the quicksand below. In our opinion, he does not sound like a barrel of laughs.

⭐ Tom Fool was once a common nickname given to a stupid man. It's a bit like how the British still call the average man Joe Bloggs, and the Americans say Joe Blow to mean the same thing.

> Knock Knock
> Who's There? Jester.
> Jester who? Jester minute,
> I can't find my keys!

PLAN YOUR VISIT 34

Muncaster Castle
Ravenglass, CA18 1RQ
www.muncaster.co.uk

📞 **01229 717614**

🕐 **Daily (summer) 10.30-18.00**
Daily (out of season) 11.00-16.00
Closed Jan

££

I want to go here ☐

TAKE A STEAM-TRAIN RIDE

...on the Ravenglass and Eskdale Railway

You might not think that steam does much apart from come out of kettles. However, in the old days it was used to power entire trains!

The Ravenglass and Eskdale Railway runs for seven miles (about 40 minutes) through some of the Lake District's prettiest valleys. You ride in an open-air carriage on a real, working miniature steam train. There are also covered carriages if it's raining – which happens quite a lot in the Lake District! The railway has a nickname, La'al Ratty, which means 'little narrow way'. It has four small working steam engines called Irt, Mite, Esk (all named after rivers) and Northern Rock.

Sticker Scores

⭐ 5 — FAT CONTROLLER

⭐ 4 — STATION MASTER

⭐ 3 — ENGINE DRIVER

⭐ 2 — GRUMPY GUARD

⭐ 1 — PENNILESS PASSENGER

Best Of The Rest

🔑 The train passes through the hidden valley of Miterdale. The river Mite, which runs through it, takes its name from an old English word meaning wee. This is a cheeky reference to its dribbly water flow!

🔑 Dalegarth is the final stop of the railway. It has a visitor centre, a shop, bike hire and a cafe. Dalegarth sits at the foot of England's highest mountain, Scafell Pike (978m high).

🔑 Boot, over the bridge from Dalegarth, is home to Eskdale Mill. Built in 1578, it is one of the oldest water-powered corn mills in England. It's *boot*-iful . . .

Fascinating Facts

⭐ The Arlesdale Railway in the *Thomas the Tank Engine* stories is based on the Ravenglass and Eskdale Line. The books feature the characters Bert, Rex, Mike and Jock, who are in fact named after . . . Irt, Esk, Mite and Northern Rock!

Top Tip
Buy an Explorer ticket for unlimited travel, and you can hop on and off at any of the line's five stations all day.

PLAN YOUR VISIT 35

Ravenglass and Eskdale Railway
Cumbria, CA18 1SW
www.ravenglass-railway.co.uk

📞 **01229 717171**

🕐 **Check website for timetables**

£ – ££

I want to go here ☐

SEE LIFE ABOARD A SLAVE SHIP

...at The Rum Story

Rum has a shameful history. The alcoholic drink used to be central to the slave trade – the shocking business of buying and selling people to work very hard in awful conditions without being paid.

The Rum Story in Whitehaven explains the town's role in the rum business in the 1700s. Slaves were captured from African villages then shipped to the West Indies. On arrival they were made to grow sugar, which was then turned into rum and sent back to the UK.

Sticker Scores

5	4	3
FAIR TRADE	FREE TRADE	MARKET TRADE

2	1
RUM TRADE	SLAVE TRADE

At the museum you'll walk through part of a re-created slave ship. You'll see how slaves were chained up with barely enough space to lie down. You're also shown a sugar factory where you learn how badly the workers were treated – if they survived the journey.

Make A Day Of It

🔑 Walk down to pretty Whitehaven Harbour, where you'll see lots of boats bobbing about in the water.

🔑 Visit The Beacon, an interactive museum on the harbour side where you can look through telescopes, present your own weather forecast, and learn about life at sea!

Top Tip

Take some time to look at the remarkable kinetic clock in the Rum Story's entrance hall. It tells the story of rum through a series of sculptures and symbols.

Fascinating Facts

★ **Up to twelve million Africans were transported across the Atlantic to be used as slaves. The late 1700s was the peak of the slave trade, with almost half a million people working as slaves in the British West Indian colonies.**

★ Some of those transported were children as young as one or two years old. On a bad voyage, it is thought that as many as one in three people would die during the crossing.

★ **The slave trade was finally abolished across the British Empire in 1833 following a campaign lasting decades and led by a man called William Wilberforce. With his health failing, Wilberforce learned that slavery would be abolished on 26 July 1833. He died three days later.**

PLAN YOUR VISIT 36

The Rum Story
27 Lowther Street, Whitehaven, CA28 7DN
www.rumstory.co.uk

📞 **01946 592933**

🕐 **Daily 10.00-16.30**

I want to go here ☐

HEAR NATTERJACK TOADS

...at Hodbarrow Nature Reserve

Natterjack toads are not quiet creatures – the male's croaky call can sometimes be heard several miles away! So in that way they're a bit like grown-ups when they're cross . . .

It's also fair to say that they're not the best-looking animals. Their backs are covered in warts and they are a murky brown-olive colour. But don't be put off – they are rare in the UK, so it's a treat to see them at Hodbarrow Nature Reserve!

The site is run by the Royal Society for the Protection of Birds (RSPB), and it's also great for spotting rare birds. Look out for the great crested grebe, which has marvellous head feathers and does an amazing mating dance.

Sticker Scores

5 — TRIUMPHANT TOAD

4 — GLORIOUS GREBE

3 — WONDERFUL WARBLER

2 — LACKLUSTRE LAPWING

1 — BIRD BRAIN

Make A Day Of It

🔑 Head to gorgeous Silecroft Beach where there are five miles of sands and shallow waters that stretch as far as the eye can see. It's a great spot for kite flying, sea fishing, paddling, strolling and horse riding.

🔑 Ride a heavy horse at the nearby Cumbrian Heavy Horse Centre. Heavy horses are breeds such as Shire, Clydesdale and Ardennes that are capable of hard tasks like ploughing, farming and boiling an egg. Actually we made that last one up!

What do toads drink?
Croaka cola!

Fascinating Facts

⭐ Natterjack Toads can darken or lighten their skin to match their environment. They do this as camouflage, to prevent other animals from spotting them and turning them into a tasty lunch.

⭐ Natterjacks also have a distinctive yellow stripe down the centre of their backs. We're not sure what purpose it serves – maybe it's a runway for flying ants?

Top Tip

See if you can imitate the loud call of the male natterjack. Say the word *rrrrip* several times in a loud, rasping voice.

PLAN YOUR VISIT 37

Hodbarrow Nature Reserve
Millom, Cumbria
www.rspb.org.uk
📞 01697 351330
🕐 Open at all times

FREE

I want to go here ☐

SEE A GIANT VIKING CROSS

...at St Mary's Church

We're not suggesting that you can see an enormous Scandinavian sulking somewhere in Cumbria. What we're talking about is the country's tallest and best-preserved cross-shaped Viking stone.

This ancient cross has stood in the graveyard beside St Mary's Church in Gosforth for 1,000 years. It's covered in carvings that show various Viking and Christian scenes. The Viking cross is over four metres high, which is taller than two really cross Vikings standing on top of each other (but less likely to attack you with an axe).

The Vikings clearly liked it around here, as they occupied the area for almost 300 years. If you fancy seeing other Viking things, head inside the church and search for the two Viking tombstones (called Hogbacks).

Sticker Scores

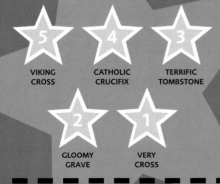

5 VIKING CROSS

4 CATHOLIC CRUCIFIX

3 TERRIFIC TOMBSTONE

2 GLOOMY GRAVE

1 VERY CROSS

Make A Day Of It

 Visit the country's highest mountain, deepest lake and smallest church all in one day – Scafell Pike, Wastwater Lake, and St Olaf's Church are all nearby.

Get your hiking boots on and head for the hills. Nearby Wasdale Head is surrounded by some fantastic peaks such as the Scafells and Great Gable.

Photo Op
Get a snap of you looking cross beside the Viking Cross. Go to town with your frown!

Fascinating Facts

★ **The World's Biggest Liar Competition is held nearby at The Bridge Inn, in Santon Bridge. The history of the event stretches back to the nineteenth century when Will Ritson, the owner of the pub, entertained his clients with tall tales. Our favourites are the one about how he had crossed foxes with eagles to make a new animal (a feagle?) and another about how he hollowed out a giant turnip to make a home for sheep!**

★ The competition is still going strong and is famous around the world. Entrants have five minutes to tell the most convincing fib! Presumably they pick the winner by seeing whose pants are on fire by the end of the night!

PLAN YOUR VISIT 38

St Mary's Church
Gosforth, Cumbria CA20 1AU
www.visitcumbria.com

FREE

I want to go here ☐

A65

A5092

A595

41
Ulverston

A590

39
A590

Dalton-in-Furness

43
Barrow-in-Furness

40
Cartmel

44
Grange-over-
Sands

45
Ravenstown

A590

A590

Milnthorpe

42

A65

Burton-in-Kendal

Camforth

M6

KEY

● Places

⌇ Lakes

WATCH A TIGER HUNT

...at the South Lakes Wild Animal Park

We don't recommend that you ever try to feed a tiger yourself – unless you want to be part of the menu. Far better to stand behind a fence and watch them hunt . . .

The South Lakes Wild Animal Park is the only place in Europe where you can see tigers hunting for food. They climb a six metre pole to grab meat that has been placed at the top. Of course, the keepers could just chuck them some grub, but this would be no fun for the tiger. Making them climb a pole also keeps the creatures fit, and copies how they'd hunt for food in the wild. It's like lunch and a PE lesson all rolled into one!

Sticker Scores

5	4	3
HEAD ZOO KEEPER	TIGER TAMER	LION HANDLER

2	1
CAGE SWEEPER	POO COLLECTOR

Best Of The Rest

🔑 There are plenty of other animals to keep you occupied – more than 150 species live here. For example, ring-tailed lemurs (like the ones in the film *Madagascar*) roam freely around the park.

🔑 How would you like to stroke a giraffe's nose? Every morning the park offers visitors the chance to feed the giraffes by hand. Check the website for feeding times. You can also help out with feeding penguins, kangaroos and emus. Very *emu*-sing.

🔑 The park takes its conservation work very seriously – two incredibly rare white rhino calves have recently been born here. You can see them either in their pens or outside in the special enclosures.

Fascinating Facts

⭐ **The park is the only place in Britain where you can see both the world's biggest tigers (Amur) and also the smallest ones (Sumatran). Enjoy them while you can, because they are endangered species.**

Lunch time!

> **What did the lion say to his cubs?**
> Don't go over the road until you see the zebra crossing!

PLAN YOUR VISIT 39

South Lakes Wild Animal Park
Broughton Road, Dalton in Furness, LA15 8JR
www.wildanimalpark.co.uk

📞 **01229 466086**

🕐 **Daily (summer) 10.00-17.00
Daily (out of season) 10.00-16.30**

£££

I want to go here ☐

TASTE THE ORIGINAL STICKY TOFFEE

...at Cartmel Village Shop

If you spend a day walking in the Lake District, you need some filling food to keep you going. So it's no surprise that local people invented sticky toffee pudding – a gooey, gorgeous, energy-giving cake!

Sticky toffee pudding is a sponge cake covered in a rich toffee sauce. While some people might disagree on the exact origins of the dessert, there's no doubt that the version sold at Cartmel Village Shop – often called the home of sticky toffee pudding – is simply sensational! Its perfect puddings are world famous, and sell to international customers in all shapes and sizes (the puddings, not the customers). After an energetic day it certainly beats a celery sandwich!

Sticky Scores

5 PROFESSIONAL PUDDING

4 SUPERB SWEET

3 CRACKING CAKE

2 DECENT DESSERT

1 TAKES THE BISCUIT

UDDING

NORTH LAKES

SOUTH LAKES

WEST COAST

SOUTH COAST

TOP FIVES

Make A Day Of It

🔑 Cartmel Priory was built by monks 800 years ago and is at the heart of the village today. Take the guided tour every Wednesday from May to October to hear why there are carvings of a monkey and a mermaid inside the church!

🔑 Cartmel also has a National Hunt racecourse, where horses race over jumps. Have a stroll over to see why some people think it is the prettiest racecourse in England.

What did the teddy bear say when offered sticky toffee pudding?

No thanks – I'm stuffed!

Fascinating Facts

⭐ **Not all desserts are necessarily bad for you. Marzipan (a sugary almond sweet) was used by doctors in the 1600s as a medicine!**

⭐ Confusingly, the word pudding means different things in different countries. In America, pudding is usually a milky dessert. In the UK, a pudding is sometimes a stodgy cake, but the word also can also be used to mean any dessert. Then there's Yorkshire pudding, which is normally served with roast beef, and black pudding, which is a blood-filled sausage! Thankfully, Cartmel tell us that blood is definitely not one of the ingredients in their sticky toffee pudding!

PLAN YOUR VISIT 40

Cartmel Village Shop
Parkgate House, The Square, Cartmel, LA11 6QB
www.cartmelvillageshop.co.uk

📞 **01539 536280**

🕐 **Mon-Sat 09.00-17.00**
Sun 10.30-16.30

£

I want to go here ☐

CLIMB UP A LIGHTHOUSE

...at the Sir John Barrow Monument

I magine that you were looking for a location to build a lighthouse. What sort of spot would you choose? Somewhere on the coast perhaps, so ships could see the light?

Well, for the Sir John Barrow Monument, they decided on a hill which is, umm, a fair way from the sea. Oh, and they didn't put a light in it . . .

The monument was actually never meant to be a real lighthouse. It was built to honour Sir John Barrow, an explorer from nearby Ulverston. You can follow in his intrepid footsteps by walking up Hoad Hill and then climbing the 112 steps to the top of the lighthouse. Take the narrow spiral staircase and enjoy the fantastic views. It's de-*light*-ful!

Sticker Scores

5 LIGHTHOUSE   **4** LIGHT BULB   **3** LIGHT LUNCH

2 LIGHTNING   **1** LIGHTS OUT

Make A Day Of It

🔑 Head to Ulverston's Laurel and Hardy Museum. It's a museum dedicated to the famous comedy double act from the 1930s and 1940s. The films may be old, but they'll still make you laugh . . .

🔑 See glass-blowing and glass-cutting at the Cumbria Crystal glass factory.

Photo Op
If you get the angles right you can take a photo which makes it look like you're leaning against the monument. Stand with the Hoad in the background and hold your hand out to give the impression that the monument is supporting your weight.

Fascinating Facts

⭐ The Sir John Barrow Monument is over 30 metres high, which is as tall as 300 light bulbs stacked on top of each other (but less illuminating).

⭐ Some people also refer to the monument as the Hoad, because it stands on Hoad Hill.

⭐ Another of its nicknames is the Pepper Pot, because of its shape. During the Second World War, the Nazis threatened to bomb the monument. Thankfully, they didn't – and the Pepper Pot became a symbol of British resistance.

What's the difference between a lighthouse keeper and a jeweller?

One watches seas, the other sees watches!

PLAN YOUR VISIT 41

The Sir John Barrow Monument
Hoad Hill, Ulverston, Cumbria, LA12
www.sirjohnbarrowmonument.co.uk

📞 01229 585697

🕐 Sun & Bank holidays (peak) 14.00-17.00
Sat (Aug) 14.00-17.00
Times may vary – check website
A flying flag on top means it's open!

FREE (donations welcome)

I want to go here ☐

BE A ZOO KEEPER FOR A DAY

...at the Lakeland Wildlife Oasis

Ever wanted to stroke a snake, look after a lemur or engage with an iguana? At the Lakeland Wildlife Oasis you can work with a real zoo keeper and look after a range of exotic animals for a morning!

The Wildlife Oasis is home to all kinds of exotic creatures. You can crawl into the meerkat enclosure, guess a fruit bat's wingspan, or stare at poison arrow frogs. South American warriors used the poisonous blood from these amphibians to make their arrow tips even more deadly.

The junior zoo keeper experience has to be booked in advance and you must be accompanied by an adult. However, don't worry if you haven't arranged anything – the Wildlife Oasis has plenty to keep non-zoo keepers occupied!

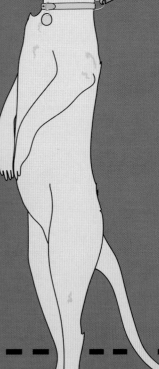

Sticker Scores

5 MEERKAT MINDER

4 BUTTERFLY BODYGUARD

3 SPIDER SUPPORTER

2 PYTHON PROTECTOR

1 ANTICLIMAX

Make A Day Of It

🔑 Grab a net and go hunting for shrimps on beautiful local beaches in the Arnside and Silverdale Area of Outstanding Natural Beauty at Morecambe Bay. But do make sure you have supervision – both beaches are known for dangerous tides and quicksand, so it's important to check first that it's safe.

🔑 See tremendous topiary at nearby Levens Hall. Topiary is the word used to describe bushes and trees that have been trimmed into interesting shapes and sculptures – and Levens has the finest topiary garden in England.

Fascinating Facts

⭐ The aquarium at Lakeland Oasis is home to mudskippers and lungfish. Mudskippers are walking fish that spend most of their life out of water and use their fins to move along on land. Lungfish haven't changed much for the last 100 million years. They breathe air and eat pretty much anything that moves. So watch your fingers!

Why do animals never play cards with big cats?

Because they are worried they might be cheetahs!

PLAN YOUR VISIT 42

Lakeland Wildlife Oasis
Hale, Milnthorpe, LA7 7BW
www.wildlifeoasis.co.uk

📞 01539 563027

🕐 Daily 10.00-17.00

£££ (junior zoo keeper)

££ (standard entry)

I want to go here ☐

99

FIND HIDDEN RUINS

...at Furness Abbey

It's hard to hide a great big building, but the monks that built Furness Abbey knew what they were doing. By selecting a secluded location, they made sure it was out of sight of dangerous thieves and attackers . . .

Furness Abbey is a beautiful, crumbling old ruin that's over 800 years old. The monks who lived there were not short of cash – as well as praying lots they also found time to be successful businessmen. They ran farms and controlled important trade routes, making Furness one of the richest medieval monasteries in England.

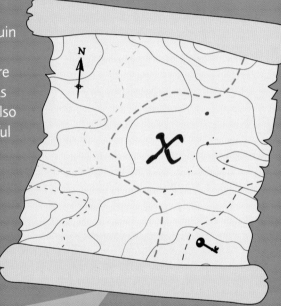

Sticker Scores

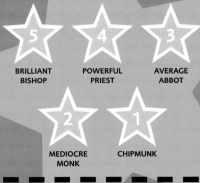

5 — BRILLIANT BISHOP

4 — POWERFUL PRIEST

3 — AVERAGE ABBOT

2 — MEDIOCRE MONK

1 — CHIPMUNK

Once you've found the abbey you can take an audio tour of it or head to the museum – just make sure you leave time to wander round the ruins!

Make A Day Of It

 Visit two nature reserves on nearby Walney Island, which is linked to the Furness Peninsula by a bridge. Bronze Age axes and arrowheads from over 3,000 years ago have been uncovered here.

 Take a ferry to Piel Island, where you'll find a cracking castle. The only people living on the island now are the pub landlord and his family. He is known as the King of Piel and has the power to knight people who buy a round of drinks!

> What is a ghost's favourite party game?
>
> Hide-and-shriek!

Fascinating Facts

⭐ **Furness Abbey is said to be haunted. Apparently, its ghosts include a murdered monk who climbs the stairs and a young girl who visits to mourn her drowned boyfriend. A headless man is also supposed to ride around on horseback. *So listen out for hooves behind you . . .***

⭐ The abbey is located in the Vale of Deadly Nightshade. While it sounds like a murderous bedside lamp, deadly nightshade is in fact a poisonous plant that used to grow at the abbey. The valley was given the name after the poison was used to murder the abbot (head of the abbey) in 1351.

PLAN YOUR VISIT 43

Furness Abbey

Near Barrow-in-Furness, LA13 0PJ

www.english-heritage.org.uk

📞 01229 823420

🕐 Usually 10.00-16.00
(Days and times vary by month)

£   ✕ (nearby pub)

I want to go here ☐

BE GUIDED ACROSS SINKING SAND

...at Morecambe Bay

The tides at Morecambe Bay can come in at the speed of a galloping horse (but without the whinnying). Many people have lost horses, tractors and even their lives on the bay's treacherous quicksand.

The good news is that you can avoid a sticky end by joining a group to cross the sands. Cedric Robinson, a local fisherman, was appointed as the 25th Queen's Guide to the Sands in 1963 and has taken groups across Morecambe Bay ever since. He reads the sands like you might read a storybook.

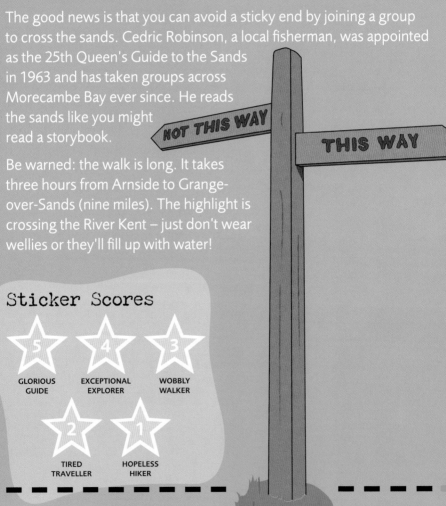

NOT THIS WAY

THIS WAY

Be warned: the walk is long. It takes three hours from Arnside to Grange-over-Sands (nine miles). The highlight is crossing the River Kent – just don't wear wellies or they'll fill up with water!

Sticker Scores

5 GLORIOUS GUIDE

4 EXCEPTIONAL EXPLORER

3 WOBBLY WALKER

2 TIRED TRAVELLER

1 HOPELESS HIKER

Best Of The Rest

🔑 Higginsons, the butchers in Grange-over-Sands, has been voted the best butcher's shop in England. Treat yourself to one of their pork pies. We're getting hungry just thinking about them!

🔑 Nearby Humphrey Head Nature Reserve has the tallest limestone cliff in Cumbria. Scramble to the top for incredible views across Morecambe Bay.

Top Tip

Whatever you do, **do not attempt to cross the bay without the official guide. The sands are treacherous** – and many people have perished trying to do so.

Fascinating Facts

⭐ **Legend has it that the last wolf in England was killed in the 1400s on Humphrey Head. (Not on Humphrey's head. We don't even know anyone called Humphrey.)**

⭐ Morecambe Bay is the largest stretch of mudflats in England and is home to all kinds of wildlife. The ground is jam-packed with juicy worms, crustaceans and shellfish. Around a quarter of a million birds munch on these nutritious titbits as they pass through the bay on their winter migration!

What do you call a wicked old woman who lives by the sea?

A sand-witch!

PLAN YOUR VISIT 44

Morecambe Bay
www.morecambe.co.uk/walk.html

📞 01539 532165

🕐 Guided walks summer only
Times vary by tides

FREE (tips welcome)

I want to go here ☐

FEED ANIMALS

...at Ducky's Park Farm

Ducky's Park Farm is a brilliant place to get up close to the animals and learn about life on a farm. You'll see some not so *farm*-iliar creatures too!

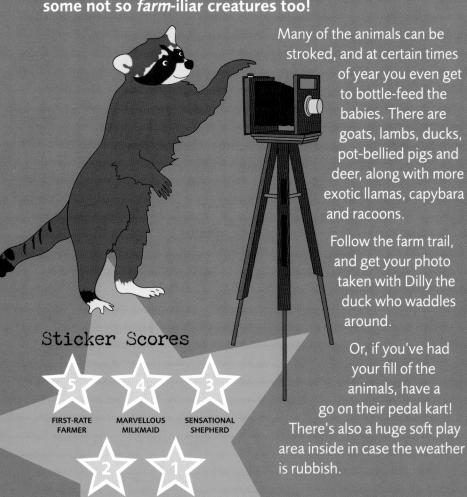

Many of the animals can be stroked, and at certain times of year you even get to bottle-feed the babies. There are goats, lambs, ducks, pot-bellied pigs and deer, along with more exotic llamas, capybara and racoons.

Follow the farm trail, and get your photo taken with Dilly the duck who waddles around.

Or, if you've had your fill of the animals, have a go on their pedal kart! There's also a huge soft play area inside in case the weather is rubbish.

Sticker Scores

5 FIRST-RATE FARMER

4 MARVELLOUS MILKMAID

3 SENSATIONAL SHEPHERD

2 GHASTLY GOATHERD

1 PATHETIC PIG KEEPER

Make A Day Of It

🔍 At nearby Holker Hall you can track down the famous Great Holker Lime in the beautiful gardens – it's one of the biggest trees in Europe and measures a whopping 7.9 metres around its trunk.

🔍 What about visiting a mini Lake District? The Lakeland Miniature Village has over 120 tiny houses, barns and farms made by hand from local slate . . . and the collection is still growing!

Why was the sheep told off?

He refused to say 'Thank ewe'!

Fascinating Facts

⭐ **Despite their reputation for spitting, llamas are friendly, gentle and clean animals. They like to come up to strangers and sniff them, and will only spit when they are extremely annoyed. So there's rarely any drama when you're near a llama!**

⭐ Llamas communicate with one another by humming and clicking. Different hums mean different things – for example, a high-pitched hum usually means they're being inquisitive. When they're scared they up the volume and let out a shrill, musical alarm.

PLAN YOUR VISIT 45

Ducky's Park Farm
Moor Lane, Flookburgh, Grange-over-Sands, LA11 7LS
www.duckysparkfarm.co.uk

📞 01539 559293

🕐 Daily (peak) 10.30-16.00
Open selected days out of season

£

I want to go here ☐

TOP FIVE

...things to spot

Car journeys can be pretty dull, but one good way to cheer them up is to take a spotter's list with you. To get you started, here are five local things to look out for.

I SPOTTED:

- [ ] Herdwick sheep
- [ ] Lakeland slate roof
- [ ] Dry-stone wall
- [ ] Daffodils
- [ ] Ghylls

Herdwick sheep

With their grey fleeces and white faces, Herdwick sheep can only be found in Cumbria.

The sheep are extremely tough and have oily wool to protect them from the freezing rain and wind. But then, as they were brought over from Scandinavia by the Vikings in the 1100s their ancestors were probably used to even worse weather! Apparently, Herdwicks normally spend their lives on the fell where they were raised. Presumably they're too *sheepish* to move!

Lakeland sl roof

Lakeland slate is a distinctive green colour and is used i houses, walls and r across Lakeland (se p15).

The slate was formed fro volcanic ash over 450 mi years ago and is a very tough building material. Presumably if it's lasted long under the ground it perfectly able to cope w a few more years on a ro Keep an eye out for it as drive along.

ry-stone all

Daffodils

Ghylls

A dry-stone wall is a wall built of ones with no mortar cement to bind em together.

know that sounds ut as sturdy as a jelly der, but trust us, it works! -stone wall building is ancient technique and uires great skill – one ne out of place and whole thing might fall r! There are thousands niles of dry stone walls oss Cumbria, so you uldn't have trouble tting one.

D affodils have been a symbol of the Lake District ever since Wordsworth wrote a poem about them (see p62).

These charming yellow flowers appear in spring and cheer up the Lake District. Why not visit the Daffodil Garden at Grasmere for a daffodil-spotter's paradise? To get you in the mood, here's a poem we wrote ourselves:

> I Will
>
> Get ill
>
> If I eat
>
> A daffodil.

A ghyll sounds like it might be a rare bird, but it is in fact a Cumbrian word for waterfall.

After a heavy rainfall, you will see ghylls spring up everywhere. They can be anything from trickles to torrents, depending on the location and the weather. However, big or small, they are an essential part of the Lake District, channelling rain water and melting snow down into the lakes below . . .

TOP FIVE

...lakes

Spending time in the Lake District and not seeing any lakes would be like going to the North Pole and staying out of the snow! There are loads of lovely lakes to choose from – here are our five favourites.

I WENT TO:

- [ ] Grasmere
- [ ] Windermere
- [ ] Derwent Water
- [ ] Ullswater
- [ ] Buttermere

Grasmere

Grasmere was Wordsworth's favourite lake – maybe it will inspire you to write some pretty poetry too!

It takes about ten minutes to walk from the village to the lake, where you can walk or hire rowing boats from the tea garden. Take a boat out and row around the wooded island in the middle. Sadly you can't land there – it's privately owned so you'll have to enjoy the view from the comfort of your boat.

Windermere

Windermere is largest natur lake in England. It's long and thin, and c map it looks a bit lik wonky blue carrot.

Because of its sheer size there's plenty to do on o around Windermere: sa fishing, canoeing, havin, a picnic, taking a ferry, climbing a fell . . . Some people even swim here, this should only be tried with supervision – and if don't mind the freezing water!

erwent Water   Ullswater   Buttermere

Derwent Water is one of the most etty and popular es. Keswick is one end and the nning Borrowdale lley is at the other.

as four islands dotted oss it which add to its uty. You can explore lake using the Keswick nch ferries. From the en landing stages u can follow footpaths ough woodland, climb to nning viewpoints or gaze aterfalls. You'll be glad u Der-*went*!

Ullswater is the second largest lake in England. It is deep and dramatic – a bit like a troubled actor!

The lake is surrounded by some of England's most famous mountains. Ullswater is known as a lake of moods because it seems to change quickly from peaceful to angry depending on the weather and the wind. Actually, that makes it sound like most grown-ups!

Buttermere is one of the western lakes. It's smaller and a bit less busy than the big, better-known ones, but no less beautiful.

The view as you approach Buttermere from the Honister Pass is spectacular. Like Ullswater, Buttermere is surrounded by mountains on all sides, and there's a beautiful mixture of farmland, woodland and fells on its banks. The valley is very narrow so the light on the lake changes constantly.

TOP FIVE

...walks

Our favourite walks include everything from short strolls to hard hikes. Just make sure you go with a good map, an adult and the right equipment (including some energy-giving chocolate and some sugary snacks!).

I WENT TO:

- [ ] Tarn Hows
- [ ] Scafell Pike
- [ ] Buttermere
- [ ] Grasmere and Rydal Water
- [ ] The Old Man of Coniston

Tarn Hows

This easy circular walk follows a gravel track around a beautiful tarn (small lake) and takes one to two hours.

Tarn Hows is one of the most famous beauty spots in the Lake District. It was created by the Victorians who joined three small tarns together. The lake is surrounded by woodland with plenty of places to play hide-and-seek, spot wildlife and build dams.

Scafell Pik

Take the tough h up Scafell Pike and you can tell yo friends that you've climbed the highest mountain in Englan

Scafell Pike is 978 metre – that's taller than 650 g pike fish stacked head t (but less smelly)! The w over ten miles and may up a full day, so you nee be properly equipped. T are several routes – our favourite starts from Wa Head car park.

ttermere

Grasmere and Rydal Water

The Old Man of Coniston

You can walk all the way around lake **t**termere on a five **l**e footpath that runs **o**ng the shores of the **k**e.

The popular lakeside trail around Grasmere and Rydal Water includes fabulous views and historic places.

Despite the name, this is not an elderly walker – it's the name of a big hill just west of Coniston village!

ttermere is one of our **o**urite lakes for lots of **s**ons (see p111). The **k** around it is reasonably **y** and takes about two **u**rs. Oh, and there are **c**es to stop for a cream **a**long the way! When **r**aining, keep your eyes **e**led for the dramatic **t**erfall at Sour Milk Ghyll.

Starting out in Grasmere village, follow the lakeshore to a small weir and footbridge. You can either continue around Rydal Water (see p64) or head back into Grasmere. Allow two to three hours for the walk – and longer if you want to hire a rowing boat or have a picnic on the way.

The walk up it is quite tough and takes four hours but is worth it for the views. You can sometimes see as far as the Isle of Man, which is 120 miles away! From Coniston village, follow the well-marked tourist route up the Old Man past Church Beck and the old mine workings.

TOP FIVE

...farms

Farming is big business in the Lake District, so it's a good place to head down to the farm and meet some animals...

Ducky's Park Farm

Ducky's is a spec-*quack*-ular place to spend the day, and has a mix of farmyard and exotic animals (see p104).

You can stroke a goat, bottle-feed a lamb and tickle a pot-bellied pig. There are also llamas, deer and capybara. Have your photo taken with farm mascot Dilly the duck who waddles around. There's a go-karting track too and if the weather isn't great you can hang out in the indoor play area.

Ducky's Park Farm
Moor Lane, Flookburgh, Grange-Over-Sands, LA11 7LS
01539 559293
www.duckysparkfarm.co.uk

Greenlands Farm Villag

Greenlands Farm Village is on th border of Lancashir and Cumbria and is home to over 120 animals including miniature donkeys, piglets and rare bre

The play barn has toy trac and bales of hay to climb you can pretend to be a fa for a day. There's also a g indoor soft play area. Oh, there's a good delicatesse butcher's shop for the gro ups to nose around in.

Greenland Farm Vi
Tewitfield, Carnforth, LA6 1JH
01524 784184
www.greenlandsfarm co.uk

alby Farm ark

Eden Ostrich World

Lakeland Maize Farm Park

Walby Farm Park near Carlisle right on Hadrian's all, just north of the ke District.

e working farm has plenty farm-iliar animals like rses, piglets and cows. wever, unlike most farms, eir outdoor play area ludes aerial slides, swings d trampolines! The indoor y area is equally impressive, d has a devilish drop slide, l pools and a wavy slide you d down on a sack.

alby Farm Park

alby, Crosby-on-Eden, Carlisle, 6 4QL

228 573056

w.walbyfarmpark.co.uk

Eden Ostrich World is a working farm set in the beautiful Eden Valley (see p30).

You'll meet a wide range of animals (not a range of wide animals) including ostriches, wallabies, spiders and guinea pigs. You can even touch and hold some of them. Look out for the ostrich incubation centre where you can sometimes see eggs hatching, and also for Pozee the zebroid – a cross between a Shetland pony and a zebra.

Eden Ostrich World

Langwathby Hall Farm, Langwathby, Penrith, CA10 1LW

01768 881771

www.ostrich-world.com

This farm near Kendal has an amazing maze made of (you guessed it) maize!

It takes about an hour and a half to two hours to complete the puzzle, and you'd better like the idea of getting lost, because that's what normally happens. Once you're done, check out the farm, which contains cows, pigs, sheep, alpacas, pygmy goats, donkeys and llamas. There are also other awesome activities including a climbing wall, indoor carting and trampolines.

Lakeland Maze Farm Park

Raines Hall Farm, Sedgwick, Kendal, LA8 0JH

01539 561760

www.lakelandmaze.co.uk

TOP FIVE

...swimming pools

You can swim in some lakes – but it's always cold and can be very dangerous so never try it without adult supervision! Instead, why not try some of these splash-tastic swimming pools . . .

I WENT TO:

- ☐ Keswick Leisure Pool
- ☐ Lakes Leisure
- ☐ The Park Leisure Centre
- ☐ The Pools
- ☐ Cockermouth Pool

Keswick Leisure Pool

We like Keswick Leisure Pool because it's got a great big water slide!

The slide is called the Black Hole and involves a slippery journey along 30 metres of winding pipes. The water in the pool is nice and warm, and you enter by walking down a gentle slope. So in some ways it's a bit like a beach in a sunny country (but without the sand).

Keswick Leisure Pool
Station Road, Keswick, CA12 4NE
01768 772760
www.carlisleleisure.com

Lakes Leisu:

Kendal is a great place for a day t and Lakes Leisure on the edge of town is v worth a visit if you fa a dip during your vis

This leisure and entertainm centre contains a 25 metre swimming pool as well as beginners' pool for childre who are learning to swim. Look out for the centre's theatre which sometimes h afternoon performances fc kids.

Lakes Leisure Ken
Burton Road, Kendal, LA9 7HX
01539 729777
www.lakesleisure.org.

he Park
eisure
entre

The Pools

Cockermouth Pool

The Park Leisure Centre has a laned wimming pool and a isure pool so both sual splashers and ness freaks are tered for.

e leisure pool has a wave chine, water cannons and a metre water slide. As well the pool, the centre contains ports hall, a gym and a cafe h a viewing area. It's also near ness Abbey, so you could mbine your visit with a stop at hidden ruin (see p100).

At most leisure centres you're lucky if they've got one pool. Here there is not one, not two, but THREE! Now that's just greedy . . .

The Pools is near the centre of Carlisle, just north of the Lake District. Its three pools are 33, 20 and 10 metres long, so there's bound to be one that's right for you. Check the website for a full timetable.

Cockermouth Pool is located just off the town's main street.

Like many leisure centres there is a good 25 metre swimming pool, a gym and sports hall. However, unlike most places they've also got a cracking climbing wall. The centre runs a children's activity programme during the school holidays including climbing, gymnastics, dance and roller skating – so it's worth calling ahead if you plan to go.

e Park Leisure Centre

eengate Street, Barrow-in-
ness, LA13 9DT

229 871146

w.theparkleisurecentre.com

The Pools Swimming and Health Centre

James Street, Carlisle, CA2 5AZ

01228 625777

www.carlisleleisure.com

Cockermouth Leisure Centre and Pool

Castlegate Drive, Cockermouth, CA13 9JR

01900 823596

www.carlisleleisure.com

TOP FIVE

...soft play areas

It rains a lot in the Lake District, but then as the locals say, 'No rain, no lakes'. Anyway, if it's chucking it down, why not head to one of these super soft play areas?

I WENT TO:

- [ ] **Fun For Kids**
- [ ] **Quayside Kids**
- [ ] **Funtazia**
- [ ] **Rheged**
- [ ] **Jordan's Jungle Fun House**

Fun For Kids

This indoor play area is big and well-named. We agree it's fun for kids!

There are plenty of things here to bounce on, climb up and slide down. There's also a snack bar where grown-ups can sit and gossip while you play on the equipment. The centre is near the Museum of Lakeland Life (see p70), so you can build it into a brilliant day out.

Fun For Kids
Parkside Road, Kendal, LA9 7DU
01539 735556

Quayside Ki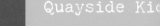

Quayside Kids is just a great pla to play – it also serv great cakes.

If you find yourself in Bowness on a rainy day, head down to the bay an you'll find Quayside Kids got climbing areas, slides tunnels and a swing ball. well as the impressive ca the café has lovely views Lake Windermere – but reckon you'll be too busy munching to notice!

Quayside Kids
The Quays, Glebe Road, Bo on-Windermere, LA23 3HE
01539 445354
www.quaysidekids.co

untazia

untazia is one of the largest play centres the Lake District.

ıere's a giant play frame th three levels to explore. u'll also find slides, ball ɔols and swings. See how gh you can climb, how r you can swing and how gh you can jump. Or just ɛt lost in their indoor maze. 'hatever you do, Funtazia ll *amaze-ya*!

ɹntazia
ıit 13, Currock Road Trade
ɛntre, Carlisle, CA2 5AD
228 409408
ww.funtazia.co.uk

Rheged

Rheged has loads to keep you busy on a rainy day (see p36) – and the indoor soft play area is particularly good fun.

You'll find tunnels to crawl through, slides to slip down and ball pools to dive into. And once you're done with all of that, you can head next door to a pottery painting workshop or step outside for the outdoor play area.

Rheged Centre
Redhills, Penrith, CA11 0DQ
01768 868000
www.rheged.com

Jordan's Jungle Fun House

Jordan's is not an actual jungle – after all, this is the Lake District, not the Amazon!

However, it is a great adventure play area in the centre of Cockermouth. As you'd expect, there are all the usual options for climbing, sliding and swinging (but not from tree to tree – we've already told you it's not a real jungle!). Check out the three-level climbing area and the open wavy slide.

Jordan's Jungle Fun House
Lorton Road, Cockermouth, CA13 9RH
01900 826115
www.cockermouth.org.uk

PARENTS' PAGE

Hey there. This is the page that's for grown-ups, not children. So stop reading if you're a child. Stop! Look, it's not for you. It says so in the title. OK, strictly speaking it says 'Parents' Page', but actually it's for all adults and not just parents. It's just that we thought that 'Page For All Adults Not Just Parents' sounded a bit rubbish. Either way, it's definitely NOT for children. So stop reading if you're a child. We really mean it. Stop. Now.

So anyway, hello, adult.

Lake District Unlocked is for children who are visiting places with adults. The sites in the book generally don't admit unaccompanied children, so we figure you're going to be the one actually planning the trip. To help you out we've included site details, such as telephone numbers and opening hours on each page. Bear in mind that most sites are closed for Christmas, and that last admission is usually earlier than the closing time. We've also specified if there are height or age restrictions. While we have tried hard to ensure all the details are accurate at the time of going to press, things change, so it's best to check before you go anywhere.

Next, the Internet. We've tried to make sure that all our listed websites are child-friendly, but all the same, we suggest you supervise any surfing. We take no responsibility for third-party content and we recommend you check a site first if you are at all unsure.

Now for some general tips:

- Quite a few venues run good workshops and activities during weekends and school holidays. These are sometimes free, but may require advance booking.

- Many of the activities can be combined into a single day out. Use the maps at the beginning of each section to work out what things are near each other.

- Some of the activities in our book could be dangerous without appropriate adult supervision. Children using this book should be accompanied at all times.

- Many of the activities involve walks, which obviously don't have opening hours as such. However, we advise that you go only during daylight and make sure you leave enough time to complete them. Check the lengths of your walk before you go to make sure it's manageable and that you wear appropriate clothing!

Great, that's the practical stuff sorted. Now, because we don't want you to feel left out, here are some facts about the Lake District that we've selected just for you. They're more boring than the facts in the rest of the book, obviously. But you're an adult, so that's the kind of thing you like.

- The Lake District is part of the county of Cumbria, which was created in 1974 when the former counties of Cumberland, Westmorland, and parts of Lancashire and Yorkshire were merged together. You probably remember when it happened. Ah, those were the days, weren't they?

- The city of Carlisle is the administrative and commercial centre of Cumbria. It is situated on the Eden River. The city was formed in 1974 and it includes the previous county borough of Carlisle, as well as the rural area bordering Scotland. The city is an important transportation centre, as well as the manufacturing hub of the county.

- The Lake District is 2,292 square kilometres in size and has a population of just over 42,000. Some of these people are adults just like you.

- The revenue generated by the tourism industry in the Lake District can be subdivided into categories. Around 28% is spent on accommodation, 28% is spent by visitor-related businesses on tourist-related goods, 18% on visitors buying food and drink, 11% on transport, 10% on shopping and around 5% on other recreation. We do not have any statistics on how much of the money was actually spent on fun stuff.

- Are you seriously going to read through all of these? Yikes We knew that adults like boring facts, but do you realise that if you turn to page 22 you can read about an enormous pencil? Oh well, suit yourself. Here's another fact . . .

- The Lake District is England's wettest region, and the average annual rainfall is over 2,000 mm. However, there is a considerable amount of local variation. For example Seathwaite in Borrowdale receives on average of 3,300 mm of rainfall a year, making it the wettest inhabited town in the United Kingdom; whereas Penrith receives only 870 mm annual rainfall. But even that's quite a lot. It's not as if Penrith has been plucked from the Sahara and plonked in Cumbria.

- The Lake District has a maritime climate, with only moderate differences in temperature throughout the year. The Lake District's valleys have an average temperature ranges of around 3° C in January to approximately 15° C in July, while the higher areas experience a bit more fluctuation in temperature.

- The Lake District is an anagram of A Restitched Kilt.

Right then, that's just about everything. Now you can give this guide back to the child you pinched it from. Or, if you're a child and you've gone through all the boring adult stuff in the hope of reading something funny, we hope you learned your lesson.

INDEX

Here's an index of all the places included

...he book, arranged in alphabetical order

INDEX

Where can you . . .

. . .be active?

. . .find animals?

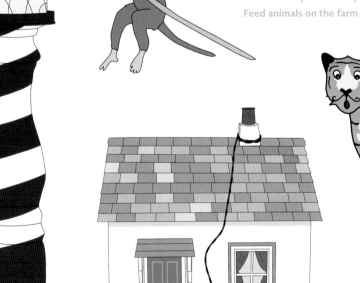

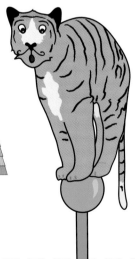

..see cool stuff?

...visit lakes and other bits of water?

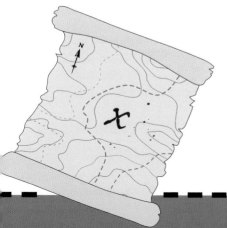

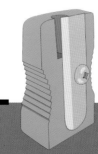

BACK-OF-THE-BOOK QUIZ

Good Luck!

The answers to all the following questions can be found somewhere in Lake District Unlocked. Email a correct set of answers to us and you'll have a chance to win a signed and framed illustration of your choice from the book!

1 Where was the last wolf in England legendarily killed?

2 How big is the Great Holker Lime (and what is it)?

3 How many million bathtubs could be filled with Rydal Water?

4 What is a liger?

5 What is England's highest mountain?

6 In Roman times, peacocks' tongues were used as . . . ?

A. A dye for making clothes brightly coloured
B. A medicine for curing sore throats
C. A tasty snack at posh dinners

7 Keswick is an old English word for . . . ?

A. Cheese Farm
B. Ostrich Farm
C. Chicken Farm

8 How heavy is the heaviest stone in the Castlerigg Stone Circle?

A. As heavy as two stegosauruses
B. As heavy as two elephants
C. Heavy? Why, I could pick it up with my left hand!

9 Ospreys only ever eat . . . ?

A. Fish
B. Other birds
C. Broccoli

10 What is the wettest inhabited town in the United Kingdom, receiving an average of 3,300 millimetres of rainfall per year?

A. Seathwaite in Borrowdale
B. Borrowaite in Seathdale
C. Thisisavery in Boringquestion

Tie-breaker

In no more than 30 words, tell us what is your favourite place featured in the book and why.

Send your answers to **quiz@unlockedguides.com**

Full terms and conditions are on our website.

ABOUT US

Deborah Done

Debs always wanted to be an author and a mum. So she's rather chuffed that she's now both. She used to visit the Lake District on family holidays, and the smell of Sarah Nelson's gingerbread has stayed with her ever since. After twelve years living in London she moved to the Lake District in 2008 and never intends to leave.

Emily Kerr and Joshua Perry

Emily and Josh went to school together. They highly recommend this as a starting point for anyone wanting to run a children's publishing company. Josh wanted to be a fireman and Emily hoped to be a Blue Peter presenter. Neither of them managed to achieve these goals, but they're OK with it now. Honest. They've both been to the Lake District a few times. Emily likes climbing fells and Josh is a massive fan of the red squirrel.

Katherine Hardy (Kardy)

Kardy always wanted to have a pet pony. That would have been more feasible if she didn't live in central London. Kardy used to go exploring in the Lake District and imagine she was in the Famous Five. Quentin Blake has described her drawings as 'strong and subtly nuanced'. This is also not a bad description of her personality.

Allison Curtis

Allison wanted to work on a farm when she was younger. That didn't happen, but she still loves the outdoors. She's been to the Lake District lots of times, and is never happier than when she's just climbed to the top of a high bit. Allison was also part of a successful world record to have the most people bouncing on space hoppers at the same time. Her cars are called Doris (the Morris) and Flossie (the Land Rover).

CREDITS

Series Editors: Joshua Perry, Emily Kerr
Design: Allison Curtis
Illustrations: Katherine Hardy

Picture Research: Katherine Hardy
Maps: Allison Curtis, with reference to OpenStreetMap – a free, editable map of the world

Thank you to ...

Debs

Thank you to . . . Joshua, my beautiful boy, for teaching me about life and for bringing me nothing but joy and smiles. Mum and Dad for introducing me to Cumbria and helping me to move here. My bro and his family for being lovely. My friends from London for supporting me when I made the move and for coming all this way to visit. My new friends in Cumbria for being so welcoming and open-hearted. Kirsty – for everything. Ian, Christine, Alfie, Angie and Lol – you know what you do. Elleray for helping children to realise life is not only about education but about adventure. The Cumbrian people for welcoming a Lancastrian incomer into their midst. The Lake District, for being endlessly beautiful and beguiling – a great place to raise a child and a great place for children to visit and explore.

Emily, Josh and Kardy

Thanks to everyone who helped us with the first one. The red squirrels (again). Allison for always getting it right. Terry for an eagle eye and marvelLous proofing. Except for that L. Vicky and Pete for great suggestions. The flickr photographers, for being generous with their wonderful photos. Kate Hughes for alleviating some serious cabin fever. John Hardy for his creative support. You, the reader, for getting this far . . . the book's nearly finished, don't worry. Cumbrian tourism websites for many of the facts on the Parents' Page. Hannah Perry for continuing to be our official legal company secretary and everything, although we still haven't quite worked out what that means.

Photo Credits